God's Rivals

WHY HAS GOD ALLOWED DIFFERENT RELIGIONS?

INSIGHTS FROM THE BIBLE AND THE EARLY CHURCH

Gerald R. McDermott

IVP Academic

An imprint of InterVarsity Press
Downers Grove, Illinois

InterVarsity Press
P.O. Box 1400, Downers Grove, IL 60515-1426
World Wide Web: www.ivpress.com
E-mail: email@ivpress.com

InterVarsity Press® is the book-publishing division of InterVarsity Christian Fellowship/USA®, a student movement active on campus at hundreds of universities, colleges and schools of nursing in the United States of America, and a member movement of the International Fellowship of Evangelical Students. For information about local and regional activities, write Public Relations Dept., InterVarsity Christian Fellowship/USA, 6400 Schroeder Rd., P.O. Box 7895, Madison, WI 53707-7895, or visit the IVCF website at <www.intervarsity.org>.

Scripture quotations, unless otherwise noted, are from the New Revised Standard Version of the Bible, copyright 1989 by the Division of Christian Education of the National Council of the Churches of Christ in the USA. Used by permission. All rights reserved.

Design: Cindy Kiple

Images: stone figure: Roberto Adrian/istockphoto.com
gold mask: Vladimir Pomorsev/istockphoto.com
mask: Stev Howkins/istockphoto.com
mask: James Hernandez/istockphoto.com

ISBN 978-0-8308-2564-6

Printed in the United States of America ∞

Library of Congress Cataloging-in-Publication Data

McDermott, Gerald R. (Gerald Robert)
  God's rivals: why has God allowed different religions? / Gerald R.
  McDermott.
    p. cm.
  Includes bibliographical references and indexes.
  ISBN 978-0-8308-2564-6 (pbk.: alk. paper)
  1. Christianity and other religions. 2. Religious
pluralism—Christianity—History of doctrines. I. Title.
  BR127.M215 2007
  261.2—dc22

                                                                    2006101564

P	19	18	17	16	15	14	13	12	11	10	9	8	7	6	5	4	3	2	1
Y	22	21	20	19	18	17	16	15	14	13	12	11	10	09	08	07				

This is dedicated to

Augustine Charles McDermott,

our first grandchild

CONTENTS

ACKNOWLEDGMENTS

I HAVE MANY TO THANK FOR THIS BOOK. I thank Roanoke College and the Institute for Ecumenical and Cultural Research for time, money and leisurely environment to start this book during a wonderful sabbatical year. Jim Lewis and the Louisville Institute provided financial support that made that year possible. Patrick Henry, director of the Institute, encouraged me to write for a larger (nonscholarly) audience. This originally started as a much larger book, ultimately unworkable for one volume; Robert Benne had the good sense to suggest I package the argument within these more digestible limits. Alan Pieratt has given me encouragement and insightful suggestions along the way. Carey Newman doesn't know it, but his searching questions helped sharpen my argument. Gary Deddo, my IVP editor, has been gracious and helpful throughout the editing process. Amos Yong provided helpful criticism. My two anonymous readers helped protect me from certain kinds of misunderstanding—beyond those which this subject and my own limitations naturally provoke. The wonderful folks in the Northampton Seminar showed me that an earlier version of this book was not as accessible as I had thought and provided some helpful suggestions along the way. As always, my wife Jean has been an invaluable source of love, friendship and ideas.

INTRODUCTION

THIS IS A BOOK ABOUT A QUESTION that is new to most of us today: Why are there other religions at all? If the true God is the Father of Jesus Christ, why did this God permit the rise and flourishing of other religions?

Although this question is new for us, it wasn't new for the biblical authors and early church thinkers. They had thought long and hard about this question, and came up with an intriguing set of answers. We have generally not recognized these answers, or if we have seen the answers, we have not imagined that they were answers to *this* question. Instead, reading with eyes that have been conditioned by the Enlightenment, we have overlooked them or dismissed them as ancient superstition.

If there is one theme, or red thread, that runs through the following chapters, it is this: the biblical authors and early church theologians saw the religions not simply as human constructions but as spiritual projects as well. The religions are living and breathing beings, if you will, that have inner souls, derived in part from spiritual entities called "gods" by the Old Testament and "powers" by the New Testament. Not every bit of every religion is spiritual or directly linked to spiritual entities, but at least some parts of some of the religions are just that.

This does not rule out the presence of goodness, truth and beauty in many of the religions for the biblical authors and early church Fathers. Nor does it mean that we cannot learn anything of value from the religions.

But it does mean that this spiritual dimension of the religions, which helps answer the question above and which has been generally ignored or dismissed in academic studies of the religions, must be taken seriously if we are to understand a biblical and early Christian view of non-Christian religions.

I am not the first to advance this argument. But while this perspective has been addressed—usually tangentially—in many articles and parts of books, I believe this is the first book-length attempt to tackle this question directly and at length. And it may be the first to find this common thread linking the biblical authors and the earliest major theologians. Much of the information I present is neither new nor startling (except to those who are not familiar with these sources), but I think this book shows lines of connection in a new light, which in turn sheds new light on the question we have posed.

Before we go any further I need to clarify something. I have posed my question in a way that will be accessible to you, my readers. The biblical authors and the rest of the ancient world, however, might not have understood talk about "other religions" as if they were distinct from other areas of life (which we call "culture" and "society" and "philosophy" and so on). They did not consider, as we have tended to believe since the Enlightenment, religion to be separate from "nonreligious" concerns. Everything in daily life and society had to do with Yahweh (in the Old Testament) or the Father and Jesus and the Holy Spirit (in the New Testament). This has implications for whether there is truth in "other religions," a subject we will take up in a few pages, and then repeatedly in this book.

If the biblical authors did not think of religion as distinct from anything at all in life, neither did they think of "other religions" as separated from true religion. By this I don't mean that they thought other religions were true, but that they typically did not even think in terms of "other religions." They saw people of other nations as following other gods and therefore failing to know the one true God. We will discuss what they meant by "other gods," but the point we need to know at the start is that the modern concept of "religion" as a domain somehow separated from the totality of life was unknown or dismissed by the ancient world. Some biblical authors might have believed there are other supernatural beings (called "gods") in rebellion against the only true God, but none thought of "religion" in the modern sense—as a belief system that is separated from the rest of life, or of rival belief systems that can be considered apart from active loyalty to or rebellion against the true God.

Yet because I am writing for moderns and not ancients, I will talk in terms of "the religions" and hope you will remember this important caveat. When I speak in this book about biblical and early church ideas about "the religions," I mean their ancient way of understanding religion as inseparable from all of life, and that no human beings in "other religions" can be considered apart from the real truths of the real God.

I don't mean to imply that all the biblical authors said the same thing, or that the theologians completely agreed on the religions. There is theological diversity in the Bible on the nature and reason for the religions, and each of the four early church thinkers I consider had different perspectives, largely related to the problems of their own cultural environments. But there is a developing argument, you might say, about the spiritual nature of the religions. By "developing," I mean it is cumulative, each chapter building on the preceding. Paul builds on what he finds in his Torah, and Justin Martyr develops what he finds in Paul and other parts of the New Testament. Irenaeus uses Justin but then goes in a different direction to try to understand historical dynamics. Clement learns from Irenaeus but innovates significantly. Origen listens to his predecessors, but adds a note of warning. While each of these four theologians has something different to say, and to some ears they might sound discordant, each voice has genuine biblical resonance. In other words, each of these early thinkers could claim, with justification, that he was teaching a biblical approach to the religions.

There are two extremes which often surface in Christian theology of the religions. One is what we might call the fundamentalist extreme. This tends to equate other religions with the demonic, suggesting that other faiths are netherworlds of unmixed darkness that should never be studied and about which there is nothing to appreciate. Christians of this persuasion think the only proper response to the religions is exorcism. Although this book highlights the biblical and early church focus on the spiritual (with emphasis on "darkly" spiritual) nature of the religions, and considers the possibility that some of the religions are animated by rebellious powers, it does not assert that this is the case for every religion, or every part of every religion. I am reminded that the history of Christianity is also interlaced with the demonic. I also highlight in these pages the biblical and early church recognition that God has left traces of his truth and beauty even in religions whose origins were problematic.

Part of the reason why many Christians today take this thoroughly negative approach to other religions is because they take a modern approach to "religion," which, as I have already suggested, separates religion from other aspects of life. These Christians can acknowledge truth or beauty in non-Christian "culture" or "philosophy," and are often quick to add that because "all truth is God's truth," God is ultimately the source of this truth and beauty. Therefore (they would say) God can show us his truth and beauty through Plato and Mozart (who were not orthodox Christians) and non-Christian scientists—but not through non-Christian religions, lest it be suggested that people can be saved through other religions.

Now, I am an orthodox Christian who believes salvation comes only through the life, death and resurrection of Jesus Christ. There is salvation in no one else (Acts 4:12). But the question of who can be saved has nothing to do with the questions of where we can find truth and where that truth came from. To restrict truth to culture and science and other areas is to use a modern definition of "religion" which the biblical authors would not recognize. They did not distinguish religion from any other area of life. There were no neutral domains that provided truth or beauty apart from the one true God.

Even we moderns recognize this at least at a tacit level. When we try to distinguish what is "cultural" from what is "religious," we often have difficulty. How can American respect for law and order, for example, be distinguished from America's Christian heritage which prized a God who revealed his laws and judgment against those who broke them? How can East Asian emphasis on respect for elders be separated from the Confucian teaching about filial piety?[1]

Religion and culture, then, are not easily separated. Even moderns (and modern conservative Christians) who think religion is separated from culture concede that many things in culture are rooted in religion or have a religious dimension. At the same time they recognize some truth and some beauty in culture. This suggests there might be truth and beauty in other religions, for two reasons: (1) much, if not all, of culture

---

[1]Some might argue that Confucianism is more ethical than religious, but the religious dimension is clear in Confucius's *Analects*. Confucius said that Heaven was the author of his virtue and object of his prayers (7.23; 3.13; 7.35) and that nature was under Heaven's control (16.8; 10.25).

is rooted in religion, and (2) if God is the author of truth, then all truth—no matter where it is found—must come, at least indirectly, from God. Another way of putting this is to say that if we see both truth and error in various cultures, we should not be surprised to see truth and error in various religions—since religion and culture are so intimately connected.

The other extreme that appears in Christian theology of the religions is what I would call "religious relativism." This is the position that every major religion is equally true and equally false, or at least similarly imperfect in their crude approximations of the divine. No one religion, as this position would put it, is more true than another. Folks who take this position also tend to say that God is not a person who has revealed himself, so we cannot know that one religion is the true one. Instead, various human societies over time have constructed their own theologies based on their own religious experience, and the latter is always so conditioned by historical particularities that no objective knowledge of the divine is possible. At best we can say that the divine exists, but we are on very thin ice when we try to say what the divine looks like.

I reject this extreme as well. The real event of Jesus of Nazareth in human history and his historically-attested death and resurrection declare to the world that God has indeed revealed Himself in definitive fashion. These events also show that we can know God by knowing Jesus Christ. And by knowing Jesus Christ, we can know something of the relative truth of other religions. (This, by the way, is the key to discerning what is true and false, right and wrong, in all the religions—by measuring them against the truth of Jesus Christ.)

Each of these two extremes would cut out significant portions of the biblical and early church approach to the religions. The fundamentalist extreme would deny that anything of value can be seen in the religions, while the religiously relativist perspective would dismiss the existence of other "gods" or "powers" as pre-critical superstition.

Neither option is open to us, since those things which both options reject are found in Scripture. The Bible attributes positive significance to some aspects of other religions, while it also points to darker powers. This is why the early church theologians could discuss the religions in both positive and negative terms.

In other words, there is tension in the Bible. There are biblical reasons for learning about and from the religions (see chap. 2). There are signs that God has used the religions to protect people from greater evil (see Clement's argument in chap. 7), and indications that the Logos has scattered seeds of beauty and truth in some of the religions (see Justin's proposition in chap. 5). There are also biblical reasons for being wary of the religions (see Origen's warning in chap. 8), because of the demonic nature of some dimensions of some of the religions (see Paul's suggestion in chap. 4). Problems come, for both biblical theology and Christian relations with non-Christian neighbors and friends, when that tension is dissolved. Either the extremes of fundamentalism and relativism resurface, or other distortions arise.

A common approach to these biblical themes in the last century has been to try to "get behind" the text to what was "really" there. For example, there is common agreement among scholars that ancient Israel believed, at least in its earlier history, in a "divine council"—other heavenly beings with whom Yahweh consulted or at least to whom He delegated certain functions. Much scholarly work was devoted to the question of which ancient Near Eastern myths this belief came from, or how it morphed over the centuries into the "myth" of rebellious gods and angels.

I am not concerned with those questions. My concern is to show that many biblical authors, in both Testaments, believed in the real existence of other beings or powers, and that the divine council is part and parcel of this belief. I am interested in the fact that they considered these powers to be involved in the genesis and ongoing existence of other religions and that the early church picked up and developed this view. In other words, I take a literary and theological, more than a critical-historical, approach. It matters less to me what critics think "really" happened than what the biblical authors themselves thought was happening.[2]

Since I believe that the Bible is the Word of God, and the Spirit therefore speaks to us through its view of other religions, I think these biblical and early church convictions cannot and should not be dismissed, and

---

[2]In later chapters I discuss briefly the influence of surrounding cultures on certain biblical authors and the development of the Bible's treatment of the divine council. But while some critics try to determine how and why these themes developed, and distinguish confidently the mythical from non-mythical, my intent is simply to note the presence of these themes and their meaning for other religions.

that they can in fact shed new light on how Christians today can understand and relate to other religions and their devotees. And, not unimportantly, they can also tell us a little something about why there are other religions at all. At the same time, like other questions such as why God permits evil, there is far more to that question that is shrouded in mystery.

Not only is there mystery, but complexity as well. I will suggest in this book that the Bible and the early church were on to something when they pointed to the spiritual dimension of all religions. But I do not want to imply that that is all there is to the religions. Human agency and imagination are also involved. As for any phenomenon, there are several levels of explanation.

Take a lie, for example. At one level, Christians believe Satan might have had something to do with it, since he is the "father of lies" (Jn 8:44). But a human being also has a will and therefore chooses to lie. If we blame Satan, we must also blame the individual. But we can also blame the surrounding culture, if at another level it reinforces the lie with what sociologists call "plausibility structures." So if there are untruths in other religions, they cannot be blamed solely on spiritual powers operating in or behind those religions. There are also real human choices and larger social forces.

This also means that religions are caused by both natural and supernatural factors. All are ultimately under God of course, as we said before when we talked about the ancient view of "religion." But even the ancients recognized that things happen not only by the permission and power of God but also by the will and imagination of human beings. The New Testament authors, for instance, said that Jesus was killed by the Romans and the Jewish leaders (Acts 2:36) but also by God's will (Rev 13:8). The natural and supernatural work together in history and in the same historical events.[3] So too in the religions. If there are supernatural causes, there are also natural causes.

While this book focuses primarily on the supernatural powers that shape and manipulate religions, I do not mean to imply that religion is

---

[3]I do not mean to suggest that the natural and supernatural always cooperate as distinct powers. Often, as in human willing, it is impossible to separate the divine from the human: "For it is God who is at work in you, enabling you both to will and to work for his good pleasure" (Phil 2:13).

the only domain[4] in which these forces operate. As Origen suggested, there may be supernatural powers at work—and in nefarious ways—in education, entertainment, politics and other kinds of culture. But this book does not discuss those possibilities.

I should also add that my treatment of these texts and issues reflects my Reformed theology. In other words, I believe in a big God who works in ways that burst all of our conceptual boxes—with contrasting approaches which sometimes seem paradoxical or even contradictory to us but which for him are no problem. Hence, the rebellion of angels who were intended to be dutiful servants was neither a surprise nor an obstacle to a God who sovereignly superintends everything for his ultimate purposes. The development of new religions that use some of his truths for purposes opposed to his declared designs—even these are woven into his ultimate design.

This also shapes my view of biblical inspiration. Because God is a big God, he can use pagan thinking to influence biblical authors in such a way that the final result in the biblical text is still exactly what he wants. If all truth is God's truth—and it is—then God can direct pagans toward light and then direct the biblical authors to use that "pagan" light in precisely the way that God wants.[5]

Finally, the reader will notice that I use the masculine pronoun for God. Rather than take undue space here to explain why, I have added an appendix at the end of the book for those who are curious.

---

[4]Because I speak to moderns in a modern context, I find it nearly impossible to avoid language that suggests religion is a domain separate from other aspects of reality—a notion inconceivable for the ancients and difficult even for moderns who consider the problem. But the reader should note my earlier qualifications of such language.

[5]I do not mean to suggest that the Bible is simply reworked paganism—only that where there are signs of influence from other cultures, God is still the final author.

THE SCANDAL
OF PARTICULARITY

Why Has the True God Come
to Only Some People at Some Times?

MARY OGBU IS A TWENTY-THREE-YEAR-OLD Nigerian mother of two. One year ago, after wandering into a Pentecostal church in her city, she became a Christian. Her three-year-old son had been very sick, and prayer by an elder at the church healed the boy. Mary believed the elder's testimony that Jesus was the Lord of all the gods, and that she must follow Jesus to be saved.

Now, however, Mary is confused. Her own mother, who is not a Christian, has asked her why she no longer makes sacrifices to the "orishas," Nigerian deities of nature and spirit. "And Mary," her mother asked, "why can't you worship both the orishas *and* Jesus?"

Mary had grown up believing that the skies and earth were full of all sorts of spirits and gods and demons. She had seen their power. People she knew had gotten sick, and some had died, after witch doctors had put curses on them in the name of those spirits and gods. Now that she was a Christian, she believed that Jesus' dying on the cross saved her from hell. But what about all the spirits and gods? Where was Jesus in relation to them? And where did they come from in the first place? Mary was confused.

Shang is a history professor in southern China. His specialty is the history of India and the Middle East. Three years ago, while studying for the second time at an American university in the Midwest, he became a Christian.

Shang had been an atheist before he came to faith. He remembers fending for himself for several years as a teenager during the Cultural Revolution because Red Guards had taken his schoolteacher parents to the countryside to work in the fields. His teachers in high school and university had said that religion is only for the weak-minded, and he believed them. Yet when he came to the American campus many years later, Christians invited him to church. The gospel sounded strange. But he was overwhelmed by the love that these Christians showed—especially when he had lost his wallet, and it was returned with two hundred dollars still inside.

Shang was persuaded that Jesus was God in the flesh two thousand years ago, but he still wondered about other religions. His wife is still a Buddhist. Is she wrong? Or is the Buddha just another version of the same god whom Jesus represents? Someday, he tells himself, he wants to study what Christian theologians have to say about these things. These questions puzzle him.

Sarah is a soccer mom in Virginia. She was raised as a Lutheran all her life, but now she has questions that no one around her, including her pastor, seems able to answer. She was particularly troubled by Christianity's limited historical reach. It didn't start until the first century C.E. What about all the people who lived before then? And further, what about the millions and millions of people who never heard the gospel? Were they all damned because they never accepted a gospel they never had a chance to hear?

Two years ago she took a course on the world religions at a local college. Just for fun, she thought. But it became a source of frustration. It wasn't the work or concepts she had trouble with—she made an A- without too much strain. The problem was that some of the world religions seemed to have some real truth. And some of the representatives of those religions who came to class were really neat people.

All of a sudden, after thirty years of accepting her faith without much question, she was disturbed. Why was Christianity relatively local? Sure, it was the largest world religion. But so many, throughout history, had not been exposed to it. Why wouldn't God have shown it to them if it was the only true religion?

And what about these other religions, which for the first time now seemed a bit attractive? Not that she would convert, but they had some real truth and beauty—along with elements that seemed really wrong and sometimes evil. If Jesus is the fullest form of God, why had God permitted these religions to rise and flourish? Where was God in all of this?

The Scandal of Particularity

All these questions have to do with what scholars have called "the scandal of particularity." This means the offense that is caused by the idea that the Christian God did not reveal himself fully in all times and places, but has restricted that revelation to certain particular times and peoples and places.

This scandal is not new. More than three centuries ago John Bunyan wondered why such a small proportion of the planet had access to the Christian gospel: "Could I think that so many ten thousands in so many Countreys and Kingdoms, should be without the knowledge of the right way to Heaven?"[1]

But this question goes back further than three centuries. In fact, Christian thinkers have wrestled with it since the beginning. This is because religious pluralism was at least as great a problem then as it is now. In its first few centuries the church was confronted by as much religious diversity as exists in a major metropolis today, and its first theologians worked hard to relate Jesus to Greco-Roman religion and philosophy. In the second and third centuries (as we shall see in the chapters that follow) Irenaeus and the Greek apologists (Justin Martyr and Clement of Alexandria) developed theologies of history and revelation that understood God to be at work in non-Christian traditions—and understood Christ, the Logos, to be teaching and saving souls outside of Israel and the church.

Dealing with the Scandal in the Past

Yet for most of the first millennium, most Christians were convinced that *extra ecclesiam nulla salus:* outside the church there is no salvation. As

---

[1]John Bunyan, *Grace Abounding to the Chief of Sinners,* ed. Robert Sharrock (New York: Oxford University Press, 1962), p. 31.

Cyprian (d. 258) put it, "You cannot have God for your Father if you don't have the Church for your mother."[2] Cyprian could say this because he shared the prevailing presumption that the gospel had been promulgated everywhere and that everyone had the opportunity to accept it. Even Augustine (354-430), who knew some African tribes had not yet heard, generally restricted salvation to the church: he believed that God had foreseen that those Africans would not accept Christ if he were offered to them.

In the second millennium attitudes began to change. Abelard (1079-1142) spoke of pagan saints such as Job, Noah and Enoch. Pope Gregory VII (d. 1085) conceded that Muslims who obey the Qur'an might find salvation in the bosom of Abraham, and St. Francis (1181-1226) referred to Muslim "brothers." Thomas Aquinas (1225-1274) introduced "implicit faith" and the "baptism of desire" for those who have not heard but would have embraced the gospel. Dante's *Divina Commedia* (c. 1314) places Avicenna, Averroes (Muslim philosophers) and Saladin (a Muslim ruler) in limbo, along with Greek and Roman sages and heroes from antiquity. Some Anabaptists (16th century) talked about an interfaith church of spiritual Semites with three covenants: Jewish, Christian and Muslim.

The discovery of the New World and its teeming millions of unevangelized souls stimulated new thinking about how non-Christians could be saved—by special illumination at the point of death, for example, or by evangelism after death. On these and other grounds, the likes of seventeenth-century Reformed divine Richard Baxter allowed for some outside the church to be saved.

By the nineteenth century Pius IX had redefined *extra ecclesiam nulla salus* to refer only to those *culpably* outside of the church. Vatican II (1962-1965) proceeded further to say that the religions contain seeds of the Word and "may sometimes be taken as leading the way *(paedagogia)* to the true God and as a preparation for the Gospel."[3]

---

[2]*Extra ecclesiam nulla salus,* "outside of the church there is no salvation" (Cyprian *Epistles* 73.21). And a note on a similar line in *Epist.* 4.4. For a more detailed treatment of this and other related texts, see Francis A. Sullivan, *Salvation Outside the Church?* (New York: Paulist, 1992), pp. 18-24.
[3]*Ad Gentes* 1.3.

More Recent Christian Thinking About the Religions

For much of the twentieth century Christian thinking about the religions was dominated by the question of salvation: can non-Christians be saved? In 1983 Alan Race developed a typology that has been used to understand this question until recently: pluralism, inclusivism and exclusivism (also known as restrictivism). Pluralism is the position that there are many saviors, and Jesus is just one of them. Exclusivists contend that Jesus is the only savior, and explicit confession of Jesus as savior is necessary before one dies.

Inclusivists maintain that while Christ is the only way to the Father, explicit knowledge of him is not. They believe "good" Buddhists can be saved by Jesus if they recognize their inability to save themselves and cry out for mercy. Inclusivists say these Buddhists are casting themselves upon Christ, who is God's mercy—but without knowing his name.

More recently this typology has collapsed, and the question of salvation has now taken a radical turn. Joseph DiNoia was the first prominent scholar to signal this new turn, and S. Mark Heim has given it its fullest explication.[4] They have argued that inclusivism is incoherent because the religions have different goals. Inclusivism seems to suggest that other religions seek a goal similar to that of Christians: union with an infinite, personal God.[5] How then is one to make sense of Theravada Buddhists, who don't believe in such a God and have no such goal?

Not only is inclusivism problematic in view of the plurality of goals in the religions, but closer inspection seems to indicate that all the religions are exclusive (restrictivist, in a sense) in their claims. That is, if we look at all the philosophical and moral and liturgical dimensions of the religions, we find they all teach that their religious goals can be met by following their religion alone—by adopting their methods during this life. Hence each religion is a "one and only," the only way to its kind of salvation. So inclusivism does not seem coherent because it assumes there

---

[4]Joseph DiNoia, "The Universality of Salvation and the Diversity of Religious Aims," *World Mission,* Winter 1981-1982, pp. 4-15; S. Mark Heim, *Salvations: Truth and Difference in Religion* (Maryknoll, N.Y.: Orbis, 1995).

[5]Of course, most inclusivist scholars are not so naive as to think that systems such as Advaita Vedanta (a Hindu philosophy) are theistic. The point that DiNoia and Heim make is that the ends of the religions are so radically diverse that it is impossible to think of them as leading by different routes to the same destination.

is only one salvation to be pursued by all the religions, when in reality there are many.

Pluralism doesn't make sense either, because it is crypto-inclusivist. It claims to believe in many goals but actually believes in only one: for John Hick, it is reality-centeredness; for Paul Knitter, orthopraxis that pursues liberation from social oppression; for Wilfred Cantwell Smith, universal common rationality and a universal quality of faith.[6] Each of these goals is very different from what real practitioners of the religions say they are about. While real believers from different religions say very different things about the divine and how to reach it, pluralists insist they are all talking about the same thing. In effect, then, pluralists deny any pluralism of real consequence. Like inclusivists, they say there is only one end for all. For example, Gavin D'Costa has shown recently that while the Dalai Lama tells the world that no religion is the best, he also believes that only his dGe lugs school of Tibetan Buddhism sees reality in its fullness, and that one can achieve the highest level of enlightenment only by Tibetan Buddhist practice.[7]

Different Salvations?

If the typology of pluralism/inclusivism/exclusivism no longer works, now what? Some Christian theologians are proposing a new way to look at whether or how non-Christians can be saved.[8] They are saying not only that the religions teach different goals or salvations, but that there may actually *be* different salvations. These different ends are not for the same person at the same time but for different people, or for the same person at different times. And this reality of different ends may be "providentially" provided by God. In other words, Theravadin Buddhists may indeed experience nirvana, and Muslims may indeed find Paradise. But they won't experience the fullness of the triune God.

---

[6]John Hick, *The Myth of God Incarnate* (Philadelphia: Westminster Press, 1977); John Hick, *An Interpretation of Religion* (New Haven, Conn.: Yale University Press, 1989); Paul Knitter, *No Other Name?* (Maryknoll, N.Y.: Orbis, 1985); Wilfred Cantwell Smith, *Faith and Belief* (Princeton, N.J.: Princeton University Press, 1979); W. C. Smith, *Towards a World Theology* (Maryknoll, N.Y.: Orbis, 1981).

[7]Gavin D'Costa, *The Meeting of Religions and the Trinity* (Maryknoll, N.Y.: Orbis, 2000).

[8]S. Mark Heim, *The Depth of the Riches: A Trinitarian Theology of Religious Ends* (Grand Rapids: Eerdmans, 2000).

So, they say, there are three types of religious fulfillment: lostness, imperfect and partial religious fulfillment through a non-Christian religion, and communion with the triune God—the last of which only Christian faith may provide.

What are we to make of this new way of thinking about whether non-Christians are saved? It seems to relieve us of the tormenting idea that all those who don't confess Jesus are doomed to eternal punishment. It also helps us explain our intuition that there are all sorts of "middle" people—those who don't reject God and in fact seem to love truth and/or God, but for many diverse reasons never reach personal faith in Christ.

On the other hand, these theologians make very little appeal to Scripture. They make philosophical and theological arguments based on the Neoplatonic Great Chain of Being and its concept of plenitude (the idea that the cosmos must have a near-infinite number of levels and degrees of happiness). They also refer to the Christian doctrine of the Trinity that functions as a "template for diversity" (since God is differentiated among three different persons with different roles, it makes sense that there would be different kinds of salvation). They refer to Dante's circles of Paradise, in which each soul receives its dearest desire and where there are degrees not only of damnation but also of salvation.

But while this new model has some resonance with what the Bible teaches, there are problems. For example, the New Testament proclaims that every human being is a sinner and needs to be reconciled with the triune God, and that apart from such reconciliation there is "gnashing of teeth" (Mt 8:11-12; Lk 13:27-28). Yet this model suggests happy reconciliations apart from Christ. The most noted of these theologians, S. Mark Heim, also implies there is knowledge of God without the mediation of Jesus. Yet the New Testament points to Jesus Christ as the source of all true knowledge of God (Jn 1:9).[9]

The principal result of the scandal of particularity has been the worry that undeserving people would be damned. Even if we agree that we

---

[9]Heim claims that "the Trinity teaches us that Jesus Christ cannot be an exhaustive or exclusive source for knowledge of God nor the exhaustive and exclusive act of God to save us." Yet Heim does not wrestle with biblical texts (e.g., Jn 1:9; Acts 4:12) that suggest that Christ is the mediator of all knowledge of God and the only savior (*Depth of the Riches*, p. 134).

are all undeserving, it still seems unfair or disproportionate that some are damned for rejecting a gospel they never had a chance to accept. Most of the debate, in other words, has focused on the question of salvation.

Other Questions

But there are other questions that the scandal has raised. One is whether God is interested in those beyond Israel and the church: Does the fact that God sent the gospel only to some people at some times in history mean that he was not interested in other people in other eras?

This book is about the answers that both the Bible and the early church gave to this and the earlier questions about salvation, particularly the question about why God allowed other religions in the first place. Many readers may be surprised to learn that (a) the biblical authors and early church thinkers struggled with these questions, and (b) they came up with some sophisticated answers.

In chapters three and four we will look at how the Old and New Testaments contended with these problems. Then we will move on to early church thinkers: Justin Martyr (chap. 5), Irenaeus (chap. 6), Clement of Alexandria (chap. 7) and Origen (chapter 8).

But before we get to the Bible's answers to these questions, let us first turn to the Bible for some surprising positions its authors take on some more general questions about the religions: whether those outside the church and Israel knew anything true about God through their religions and, more provocatively, whether God's people had anything to learn from people outside the church and Israel.

2

Not Even in Israel Have
I Found Such Faith

Surprising Knowledge of God Among
Bible People Outside Israel and the Church

ONE DAY JESUS PAID A VISIT TO NAZARETH, his hometown. This was at the beginning of his public ministry. On what was probably a hot Palestinian Saturday, he stood up in the synagogue and proclaimed that he was the Messiah figure of whom Isaiah prophesied (Lk 4:14-30; cf. Is 58:6; 61:1-2).[1] He was greeted with derision.

"Isn't this Joseph's son?" his Jewish neighbors asked skeptically. They demanded that he do miracles as he had done in Capernaum. Jesus replied, "Truly I tell you, no prophet is accepted in the prophet's hometown. But the truth is, there were many widows in Israel in the time of Elijah, when the heaven was shut up three years and six months, and there was a severe famine over all the land; yet Elijah was sent to none of them except to a widow at Zarephath in Sidon" (Lk 4:24-26). Jesus' neighbors were enraged. "They sprang to their feet and hustled him out of the town; and they took him up to the brow of the hill their town was built on, intending to throw him down the cliff" (Lk 4:28-29 JB). Miraculously, Jesus was able to elude their clutches.

Why were they enraged? His claim to be a messianic figure probably puzzled them. But it wasn't until he implied that some pagans were closer to God than they—the Chosen People—that they tried to kill him.

Let me explain why I say "pagans." The widow at Zarephath in Sidon

---

[1]All biblical quotations are from the New Revised Standard Version unless otherwise noted.

was a Gentile, which means one of "the nations," the non-Jews typically considered by Jews to be outside God's love. Zarephath was on the Phoenician coast south of Sidon, in the heartland of the Baal cult (see 1 Kings 16:31). That region was pagan[2] territory. Jews assumed that all its residents were far from God, probably hated by God.

The Sidonian woman Jesus referred to had only a handful of meal, but when the prophet Elijah commanded her to make a cake out of it, she proceeded to bake, trusting Elijah's promise that God would miraculously multiply the meal (1 Kings 17:1-16). Of course, she was also desperate and had nothing to lose, since she and her son were doomed to die soon with or without the handful of meal. But Jesus commended her nonetheless, because of her faith in Elijah's word, which was the word of the Lord. She had less evidence for faith than the residents of Nazareth had, but she believed that God was speaking and could be trusted.

Notice that Jesus here praised the faith of a pagan and suggested that her faith was better than the faith of his Jewish neighbors.[3] This surprises most readers, especially those who have assumed that the Bible has only negative things to say about those who believe in other religions. This little story is just one illustration of a startling feature of the Bible—that it has more to say on pagans than most of its readers have realized.

Now plenty of what the Bible has to say about other religions is negative. Many readers are familiar with its denunciation of pagan idolatry and its warnings to the Jews to avoid it. The Ten Commandments forbade it: "You shall not make for yourself an idol . . . you shall not bow down to them or serve them" (Ex 20:4-5 RSV). When the Jews started worshiping the gods of the nations, the prophets were quick to condemn their stupidity and betrayal of Israel's God (Is 40:18-20; 46:1-2, 5-7; Jer 10:3-4; Ezek 7:20; 8:10). The New Testament also proscribes pagan idolatry, both in Greco-Roman religions (Acts 7:43; 15:20; 17:29; Rom 1:23) and in the Roman emperor cult (Mk 13:14).

But the Bible is full of surprises. For example, it suggests repeatedly

---

[2]In this book *pagan* will be used to refer to people who were or are neither Jewish nor Christian. Nothing demeaning is intended by the use of this term.

[3]Jesus praises her faith, not her pagan religion. Jesus clearly believed that the Jewish religion, as presented in the Torah (the Old Testament), was true and that pagan religions were not. See, for example, his statement that "salvation comes from the Jews" (Jn 4:22).

that people outside the Jewish and Christian traditions have knowledge of God and that God's people have learned from other traditions. Even the Bible itself shows signs of influence from other religious cultures.

God Wants the Gentiles to Know Him

A recurring theme in the Old Testament is that Yahweh wants all the world to know that he is the Lord. It is prominent even in the story of the Exodus, where God is concerned not only with redeeming his own people but also with displaying his glory to everyone else—particularly the Egyptians. In other words, he is intent on showing his salvation not only to the Jews but also to their captors: "I will harden Pharaoh's heart, and he will pursue [the Israelites], so that I will gain glory for myself over Pharaoh and all his army; and the Egyptians shall know that I am the LORD" (Ex 14:4; cf. Ex 14:18). In the greatest act of salvation of the pre-Christian era, God wanted not only to save the Jews but also to reveal who he is to the Gentiles.

The same theme surfaces again in the prophets, particularly Isaiah and Ezekiel. In Isaiah 37, King Hezekiah prays that Yahweh would save Judah from capture by the Assyrian king Sennacherib: "So now, O LORD our God, save us from his hand, so that all the kingdoms of the earth may know that you alone are the LORD" (Is 37:20). Hezekiah suggests that it is God's desire for all the kingdoms of the world to know him, or at least to acknowledge his sovereignty, and that an answer to his prayer will fulfill that desire. Later Isaiah foretells a time when all people together shall see the glory of the Lord, and the suffering servant will bring light and justice to the nations (Is 40:5; 42:1; 49:6). God's punishment of Zion's oppressors will show "all flesh" that the Mighty One of Jacob is her Savior and Redeemer (Is 49:26). Both Isaiah and Jeremiah proclaim that the nations shall come to the light of Jerusalem and gather before the throne of the Lord (Is 60:3; 66:18-19; Jer 1:5; 3:17).

Ezekiel addresses the nations more specifically on this score. In general, he announces, God wants his name not to be profaned among the nations, but to manifest his holiness in the sight of the nations, and for all flesh to know that he is the Lord (Ezek 20:9, 14, 22, 41; 21:5). More directly, he declares that through his chastisements the following peoples will discover that he alone is God: the Ammonites, Moabites, Phi-

listines, residents of Tyre and Sidon, and the Egyptians (Ezek 25:5, 11,
16-17; 26:4-6; 28:22-23; 29:6, 8, 16; 30:19, 26; 32:15). He tells Gog, the
ruler and general of Magog's forces,[4] that he will use him to invade Israel
"so that the nations may know me, when through you, O Gog, I display
my holiness before their eyes" (Ezek 38:16). In the same chapter God
adds that he will also destroy Gog, and that even that destruction "will
display my greatness and my holiness and make myself known in the
eyes of many nations. Then they shall know that I am the LORD" (Ezek
38:23).

We are told through these passages, then, that the history of salvation
in the Old Testament is not simply a story of God's raising up and deliv-
ering a people for himself through Israel; it *is* that, of course, but that
history was not conducted in utter disregard for the nations that surrounded Israel. God was also intent on making himself known to those
surrounding peoples. We don't know if these other peoples would be
saved through this knowledge. But we do know that God intended not
only to save the Jews, but also to make known his name and glory to
Gentiles throughout the ancient Near East. This means that some Gentiles outside of Israel came to know something of the true God through
what God did in and through Israel.

The New Testament also intimates that God wants to reveal himself
to men and women outside the orbit of the Christian revelation. Paul
tells the Romans that in fact God has *already* revealed himself to every
human being: God's existence and nature and power can be known to
all through nature ("what has been made"), and his holy law has been
written on every human heart (Rom 1:19-20; 2:14-15). Acts 14:17 states
that God witnesses to himself through the blessings of nature and food:
"he has not left himself without a witness in doing good—giving you
rains from heaven and fruitful seasons, and filling you with food and
your hearts with joy."

We see, then, that God is portrayed by Scripture as wanting to reveal
himself in ways not connected to the history of Israel or Christ. These
ways of revelation seem to spring from a desire to make himself known

---

[4]"Gog and Magog appear [to be] transhistorical, though the name Gog may derive from the
name of the Lydian ruler Gyges." David L. Petersen, notes to Ezekiel, in *The HarperCollins
Study Bible*, ed. Wayne A. Meeks (New York: HarperCollins, 1993).

even to people who have not heard of the revelation in Israel and Christ.

Knowledge of God Outside the Hebrew and
Christian Traditions

If Scripture suggests that God *desires* the entire world to know him, it also indicates that people outside the Jewish and Christian communities *have* known at least some aspects of his person and character. For example, the early pages of the Bible contain the remarkable story of Melchizedek, a Canaanite priest-king who is shown to have known the true God but apart from the revelation given to Abram (Gen 14:17-24). Melchizedek, whom the author of Genesis calls the king of Salem (identified with Jerusalem in Ps 76:2), brought bread and wine to Abram after his victory over Chedorlaomer and his allies. The text says that Melchizedek was a priest of El Elyon (roughly translated "God Most High"), a Canaanite deity whose identity here is curiously merged with Abram's God.

Melchizedek blessed Abram by El Elyon, and said El Elyon is maker of heaven and earth (Gen 14:19). Then Melchizedek blessed El Elyon and declared that El Elyon had delivered Abram's enemies into his hand (Gen 14:20). Abram then tithed to Melchizedek. When another figure in the story, the king of Sodom, offered to Abram the spoils taken from the defeated armies, Abram refused with these intriguing words: "I have sworn to Yahweh El Elyon, maker of heaven and earth, that I would not take a thread or a sandal-thong or anything that is yours, so that you might not say, 'I have made Abram rich'" (Gen 14:21-23).

Notice what Abram had done in these words: he identified Yahweh with El Elyon in two ways. He has joined the two names in a gesture that suggests they point to the same God, and—as if it were not completely clear—he has given Melchizedek's description of El Elyon to Yahweh: maker of heaven and earth. One distinguished Old Testament scholar argues that both Abram's acceptance of Melchizedek's blessing and his tithe to the Canaanite priest indicate that Abram acknowledged the legitimacy of Melchizedek's priesthood and sanctuary.[5]

Do you see how remarkable this is? Melchizedek is shown to be wor-

---

[5]Claus Westermann, *Genesis: A Practical Commentary* (Grand Rapids: Eerdmans, 1987), p. 115.

shiping the true God under the name of a Canaanite deity. Another way of putting this is to say that Melchizedek had knowledge of the true God despite all appearances of *not* having received revelation from the Hebrews. This is not to suggest that Melchizedek's beliefs about God were the same as Abram's, and it certainly does not imply that all Canaanite beliefs about El Elyon were accurate. But the text *does* seem to imply that Melchizedek had some sort of knowledge of the God who manifested himself as the Holy One of Israel. It means that true knowledge of God came to Melchizedek apart from revelation given through the Abrahamic lineage.

The Old Testament is full of Gentiles who knew something of the true God. Pharaoh's magicians, for example, told Pharaoh after the (third) plague of gnats, "This is the finger of God" (Ex 8:19). There is no indication that they had saving knowledge of God, but the text states that they recognized at this point that he, and not some other agent, was at work. Although the New Testament condemns Balaam's errors (2 Pet 2:15; Jude 11), the Old Testament historian records that Balaam made accurate prophecies of the future of Israel, presumably under the inspiration of the Holy Spirit (Num 24). Rahab the Canaanite prostitute recognized that the God of the Israelites was the true God, and she became an example of faith for Jewish Christians in the New Testament era (Josh 2:10-11; Heb 11:31). King Huram of Tyre told Solomon that he knew it was the God of Israel who made the heaven and the earth (2 Chron 2:11-12). Other people outside the Jewish tradition who knew and sometimes "walked with" the true God were Abel, Enoch, Noah, Job, Abimelech, Jethro, Ruth, Naaman and the Queen of Sheba.

The Old Testament is also run through as by a red thread with foreign officials recognizing the sovereignty of the God of Israel. Pharaoh, for example, more than once acknowledged that he had sinned against Yahweh (Ex 9:27; 10:16). After Naaman's healing he confessed, "Now I know that there is no God in all the earth except in Israel" (2 Kings 5:15). Nebuchadnezzar made a similar confession after Daniel interpreted his dream, and then again after Shadrach, Meshach and Abednego emerged unscathed from the fiery furnace. Then when he gained his sanity after mental illness, he again testified to the sovereignty of the God of Israel (Dan 2:46-47; 3:28; 4:34-37). When Daniel was saved from the lions, Darius issued a decree commanding "all people and nations of every language throughout the whole world" to tremble and fear before the God of Daniel: "For he is the living God, enduring forever. His kingdom shall never be destroyed, and his dominion has no end. He delivers and rescues, he works signs and wonders in heaven and on earth; for he has saved Daniel from the power of the lions" (Dan 6:25-27).

Many of these Gentiles came to know certain things about the true God only by contact with Jews. And some of them, such as the Pharaoh's magicians and Balaam, may never have come to a saving knowledge of Yahweh. Yet they nevertheless knew something about the true God. They were Gentiles outside of Israel who nonetheless knew something of the God of Israel. What they knew was not part of general revelation,[6] since it was not given to all, nor was it special revelation,[7] since it usually did not point to salvation.[8] But it was true knowledge of the true God, given by God directly or through an encounter with God's works.

The New Testament adds an intriguing twist. John indicates cryptically that the second person of the Trinity is responsible for knowledge of God given to Gentiles and non-Christians: "What has come into being in him was life, and the life was the light of all people" (Jn 1:3-4). Since John says here that all human beings have been given light by Christ, then the knowledge of God which they possess must be included in that light. It is Christ, then, who is responsible for whatever knowledge of the true God is found outside of Judaism and Christianity. John goes on to say the same thing in a slightly different way: all true enlightenment—which must include that of pagans since it is said to come to "everyone"—comes from Christ: "The true light, which enlightens everyone, was coming into the world" (Jn 1:9).

This means that Christ gave true knowledge of God to Epimenides and Aratus, the sixth and third century B.C.E. poets whom Paul quoted approvingly at Athens: "'In him we live and move and have our being'; as even some of your own poets have said, 'For we too are his off-

---

[6]This is the idea in theology that God has already revealed himself to all people (thus "general") through nature (e.g., Rom 1:18-20) and conscience (Rom 2:14-15).
[7]This means the revelation of God's saving plan through Israel and Jesus Christ, made not to every human being but to many. Perhaps because this revelation is not given universally but came at special times and through special nations and persons, it is called "special."
[8]For some like Rahab, however, it may have.

spring'" (Acts 17:28). If nothing else, this passage shows that for Luke and Paul, these secular poets possessed religious truth. They knew something about the true God. And according to John, this knowledge was mediated to Epimenides and Aratus by Christ.

God's People Learn from Those Outside the Jewish and Christian Churches

We have seen that the Bible contains surprises. It says that God not only wanted Gentiles and non-Christians to know him, but that some actually did come to know certain aspects of his person and character. Some came to this knowledge independently of Israel and the church, while others came to see something of God through God's dealings with Israel. Two Hellenistic poets are said to have known something true about God, and there is no indication that they had any knowledge of the Jewish tradition. These individuals may not all have had saving knowledge of God, but their knowledge was *true* knowledge. They had come to know something true about Yahweh, *the* Father of Jesus Christ. Now in this last section of this chapter I want to show that some of God's people in the Bible learned from pagans things that helped them better understand God's revelation through Israel and the church.

The first thing we need to understand here is that much of the religion of the patriarchs was shared by their compatriots in the ancient Near East. In fact, "there was not much in the world-view of the patriarchs and their families that differentiated them from the common ancient Near Eastern culture of the day."[9] Now this is not by itself proof that the patriarchs borrowed their religious ideas from their pagan neighbors. But there is evidence that the biblical God used pagan religion as a background from which to teach his people about true religion.

For example, in the massive polytheistic systems of the ancient world, the great cosmic deities, while respected and worshiped in national and royal contexts, "had little personal contact with the common people." In Mesopotamia in the first part of the second millennium B.C.E. people began to relate to minor deities who were thought of as "personal gods"

---

[9]John H. Walton and Victor H. Matthews, *The IVP Bible Background Commentary: Genesis-Deuteronomy* (Downers Grove, Ill.: InterVarsity Press, 1997), p. 15.

that took interest in a family or individual. While the personal deity was not worshiped exclusively, most individual and family worship was devoted to such a deity. Some scholars believe that Abraham's first responses to Yahweh may have taken place in this context: "Abraham may have viewed Yahweh as a personal god that was willing to become his 'divine sponsor.'"[10] The point is not that Yahweh took on all the characteristics of these personal gods, but that Abraham may have used this religious framework to understand Yahweh, and that Yahweh in turn may have used and then adapted this framework to teach Abraham truths about himself.

Circumcision and the smoking firepot and blazing torch in Genesis 15 are more examples from the patriarchal period. Mesopotamian religious rituals already used sacred torches and censers in rites of initiation and purification; torches and ovens represented deities. Circumcision was practiced widely in the ancient Near East as a rite of puberty, fertility or marriage. Once again, the point is that God used common cultural (and religious!) practices to teach new religious concepts about himself and his ways to his people.[11] There were symbols in these pagan practices and beliefs that God used to teach new truths, and in the process he changed the old beliefs and practices, giving them new meanings. Yet the fact remains that God's people learned things about the true God from those who had not received the fullest revelation (at the time) about that God.

Even God's names in the Bible bear mute witness to this phenomenon of learning from pagans things about the true God. The Hebrews appropriated the Semitic name *El* for God, perhaps from the Canaanites, while the New Testament authors used the Greek term *theos*. The *El* of the sixth-century B.C.E. history of Phoenicia by Sanchuniathon was a fierce warrior god—in most respects unlike Yahweh, but like Yahweh a god of

---

[10]The quotations in this paragraph are taken from a discussion of Abraham's religion in Walton and Matthews, *IVP Bible Background,* pp. 36-37. For further discussion of the influence of ancient Near Eastern culture on the Old Testament, see W. Robertson Smith, *Lectures on the Religion of the Semites,* 2nd ed. (London: A. & C. Black, 1894; Sheffield: Sheffield Academic Press, 1995); Meredith G. Kline, *Treaty of the Great King* (Grand Rapids: Eerdmans, 1963); Jack Finnegan, *Myth and Mystery: An Introduction to the Pagan Religions of the Biblical World* (Grand Rapids: Baker, 1989); James B. Pritchard, ed. *Ancient Near Eastern Texts Relating to the Old Testament,* 3rd ed. (Princeton, N.J.: Princeton University Press, 1969).

[11]Walton and Matthews, *IVP Bible Background,* pp. 42, 44.

battles.[12] The Hellenistic *theos* was often conceived as a single godhead behind many names and mythologies, or an impersonal One behind all that is.[13] The New Testament's *theos* is the epitome and source of personhood, unlike its Hellenistic counterpart, but like its namesake it is the ground and force behind everything that exists.

My point is that even when a word is borrowed and invested with new meaning, it seems impossible to strip the word of every last bit of its old meaning or context. For Christians who believe that God's Spirit superintended the entire process of Scripture writing, which included the use of language and stories used to describe other gods, this is neither surprising nor theologically problematic. It simply means that God used all of the biblical authors' influences to reveal aspects of his being and work.

It should be clear by now that the biblical authors were not always concerned about the religious or moral character of those from whom they learned. Balaam spoke the truth about the future of Israel despite becoming a symbol of avarice and idolatry. Neco, the king of Egypt, was never distinguished by moral or religious virtue. Yet the Bible says that God spoke through him and that God was displeased that Josiah did not listen to the word of the Lord that came through this pagan king (2 Chron 35:20-24).

Although there is no clear proof, evidence exists nonetheless that the author of Psalm 104 may have learned from the Egyptian hymn of Amenhotep IV (Akhenaten, early 14th century B.C.E.). This is a hymn of praise to the deity that is manifested by Aten, the sun disk. It is a remarkable example of monotheism, made all the more remarkable by its presence in a long history of ancient Egyptian polytheisms. Perhaps for this reason it vanished as soon as its progenitor died. But it contains remarkable parallels to Psalm 104. Both speak of God sending rain to water the earth and satisfy the beasts of the field and birds of the air, of the earth returning to darkness and lions emerging when the sun retires, of God's manifold works fulfilling the divine will, of ships and fish sporting in the

---

[12]Patrick D. Miller Jr., *The Divine Warrior in Early Israel* (Cambridge, Mass.: Harvard University Press, 1973).

[13]See "Theos," in *New International Dictionary of New Testament Theology,* general ed., Colin Brown, (Grand Rapids: Zondervan, 1976), 2:66-67.

oceans before God, of humans getting their food from God, and of all creaturely life depending on the divine spirit.[14]

Scholars debate the connection between the Aten hymn and Psalm 104. Some argue that the differences are more striking than the similarities. For example, the Aten hymn portrays night and the lions as almost enemies of human beings, while the psalmist sees them as "fellow-pensioners."[15] The elements that are similar are arranged in different order in each poem, and some of the most vivid images (Aten's care for the embryo of the baby in the womb and the chick in the egg) are missing from the Hebrew stanzas. Others postulate that both poems share a common background, noting general similarities with other Egyptian sun hymns and a Mesopotamian hymn to Shamash. Many believe that there was a chronological and cultural bridge between the texts—that the Aten hymn was known to Israel via Canaanite, specifically Phoenician, translations and adaptations.[16]

One of two possibilities seems likely: either these ideas were common to the ancient Near East and the psalmist used them, under the inspiration of the Holy Spirit to describe Yahweh's providence, or there was direct borrowing from the Egyptian hymn.[17] In either case non-Hebrew sources influenced the Hebrew writer in ways that eloquently depicted God's loving care for his creatures. This is part of the larger pattern that we are seeing in this chapter—God's use of non-Hebrew and non-Christian cultures to make himself known to the biblical authors. As C. S. Lewis put it,

It is conceivable that ideas derived from Akhenaten's system formed part

---

[14]For Akhenaten's hymn, see "The Hymn to the Aton," in *The Ancient Near East,* vol. 1: *An Anthology of Texts and Pictures,* ed. James B. Pritchard (Princeton, N.J.: Princeton University Press, 1958), pp. 226-30.

[15]C. S. Lewis, *Reflections on the Psalms* (Glasgow: Fontana, 1958), p. 76.

[16]See A. Barucq, *L'expression de la louange divine et de la prière dans la Bible et en Égypte,* Bibliothèque d'Étude Tom. 33 (Cairo: Institut Français d'Archéologie Orientale, 1962); K.-H. Bernhardt, "Amenhophis IV and Psalm 104," *Mitteilungen des Instituts für Oreintforschung* 15 (1969): 193-206; P. C. Craigie, "The Comparison of Hebrew Poetry: Psalm 104 in the Light of Egyptian and Ugaritic Poetry," *Semitics* 4 (1974): 10-21; G. Nagel, "À propos des rapports du Psaume 104 avec les textes égyptiens," in *Festschrift A. Bertholet,* ed. W. Baumgartner et al. (Tübingen: J.C.B. Mohr, 1950); Leslie C. Allen, *Psalms 101—150,* Word Biblical Commentary 21 (Waco, Tex.: Word, 1983), pp. 28-31.

[17]The Egyptians could not have borrowed from the psalmist because the Egyptian hymn dates from several centuries before the writing of the psalms.

of that Egyptian 'wisdom' in which Moses was bred. Whatever was true in Akhenaten's creed came to him, in some mode or other, as all truth comes to all men, from God. There is no reason why traditions descending from Akhenaten should not have been among the instruments which God used in making Himself known to Moses.[18]

Proverbs 22:17—24:22 is another example of an Old Testament text which many scholars think was influenced by a non-Hebrew tradition. A leading New Testament scholar asserts that "it is well-known" that this text is "most probably drawn" from an earlier Egyptian wisdom tradition known as the *Teaching of Amenemope*.[19] There are "striking similarities" in both structure and subject matter. Both consist of thirty precepts or exhortations. The preamble of the Proverbs passage appears in a different form in the conclusion of *Amenemope*. More than a few exhortations use the same images. For example, Proverbs 23:4-5 ("Do not wear yourself out to get rich. . . . when your eyes light upon [riches], it is gone; for suddenly it takes wings to itself, flying like an eagle toward heaven") is matched by parts of the seventh chapter of *Amenemope* ("Cast not thy heart in pursuit of riches. . . . [Or] they have made themselves wings like geese and are flown away to the heavens").[20] Another scholar says there is no way to prove direct literary dependence of the Proverbs text on the (probably) earlier Egyptian text, but thinks that the profession of scribe in that era was international, and that scribes probably were trained in a wide range of wisdom writings. If the Hebrew scribe did not have the Egyptian text before him or was not recalling it from memory, he probably was calling upon a tradition that was international rather than merely Hebrew.[21]

We see a similar pattern in the New Testament. We have already seen that Jesus commended a pagan woman on his visit to Nazareth. But it

---

[18]Lewis, *Reflections,* 74. Lewis refers to the Jewish (and early Christian) tradition that Moses "was instructed in all the wisdom of the Egyptians" (Acts 7:22). Lewis's understanding of revelation is similar to mine: God uses the whole person of the biblical author, including his religious training, to communicate divine truth through what finally winds up on the biblical page.

[19]James D. G. Dunn, "Biblical Concepts of Revelation," in *Divine Revelation,* ed. Paul Avis (Grand Rapids: Eerdmans, 1997), p. 7.

[20]"The Instruction of Amen-em-opet," in Pritchard, *The Ancient Near East,* pp. 237-43.

[21]R. B. Y. Scott, *The Anchor Bible: Proverbs and Ecclesiastes* (Garden City, N.Y.: Doubleday, 1965), pp. 20-21.

wasn't only the widow whom Jesus praised. He also lauded another pagan exemplar of faith, Naaman the Syrian general. Naaman trusted the prophet Elisha's word from God that he (Naaman) would be cured of his leprosy if he would dip himself in the Jordan River (2 Kings 5:1-14). Jesus said, "There were also many lepers in Israel in the time of the prophet Elisha, and none of them was cleansed except Naaman the Syrian" (Lk 4:27). Jesus suggested that Naaman the pagan had more faith than his Jewish contemporaries, and that his boyhood Jewish neighbors would do well to learn from this pagan. From the context it also appears that Jesus was contrasting Naaman's humility (doing what at first he considered ridiculous) with Nazareth's pride. Jesus' reference to the "oppressed" and "blind" (Lk 4:18) suggested that his hearers needed to acknowledge their sins and need for help. But in their rage they refused to humble themselves and instead tried to murder Jesus (Lk 4:28-29).

Most readers of the New Testament are also familiar with the story of the centurion who sought healing for his slave (Lk 7:1-10). When Jesus came near, the Roman soldier sent friends to tell Jesus not to bother coming any further because he was confident Jesus could heal his slave from a distance merely by uttering a word. Jesus was "amazed" by this faith response, and told his hearers, "I tell you, not even in Israel have I found such faith" (Lk 7:9). This is a third instance, then, when Jesus praised the religious example of a pagan and suggested that Jews could learn from that example. Luke seems to be suggesting that we Christians can also learn from these pagans.

Am I minimizing the centurion's faith, however, by calling him a pagan? After all, he had faith in Jesus, which he demonstrated by recognizing Jesus' authority. And he was a friend of the Jews, one who "feared" God, like Cornelius in Acts 10:2, 22. Despite these indications that he was not your ordinary pagan, we should remember that as a Roman officer, he was not permitted by Rome to undergo circumcision as a convert. Jesus himself placed him outside the Jewish community ("not even in Israel have I found such faith"). And all we know from the text is that the centurion had faith that Jesus could heal. As far as we can tell, the centurion may only have known Jesus as a miracle-worker. There were others in this part of the world whom people believed capable of such things (see Acts 8:9-11); there is no evidence that the centurion knew anything more about Jesus than that he was a worker of such wonders. Therefore it is likely that the centurion knew little more than his other pagan neighbors and acquaintances knew about Jesus—which further reinforces Jesus' (and Luke's) suggestion that we should learn from this one who was neither Jew nor (yet) Christian.

On at least three other occasions Jesus lauded the example of "pagans." Jesus celebrated the faith of the Canaanite woman in Matthew 15:21-28, recommended the ethical behavior of the Good Samaritan (Lk 10:25-37), and pointed out that "a foreigner" was the only leper among ten to "return and give praise to God" (Lk 17:18). In all three instances Jesus applauded the acts of faith made by people who were not yet inside the Jewish or Christian circles of faith, and recommended his hearers to learn from their example.[22]

Peter also seems to have learned from the religious experience of someone who had not yet been introduced to the gospel. He appears to have learned something new and profound about God from what he observed God to be doing in and for Cornelius before Cornelius heard about Jesus. When he heard that Cornelius had heard from an angel to come to the home where Peter was staying, Peter's eyes were suddenly opened to God's ways with the Gentiles: "[Now] I truly understand that God shows no partiality, but in every nation anyone who fears him and does what is right is acceptable to him" (Acts 10:34-35).

Cornelius, like the Roman centurion of Luke 7, was one of the Gentiles whom Luke several times calls seekers who feared or worshiped God (Acts 13:16, 26; 16:14; 18:7) but may not have become actual converts to Judaism. In any event, Cornelius had never heard of Jesus when he had the experience with the angel that led Peter to understand God's work of redemption in a whole new way. Later, when Cornelius heard the gospel and the Holy Spirit "fell upon all who heard the word" with him, Cornelius understood even more about this work of redemption. But the initial revelation came while he was still in his pre-Christian state—that is, while Cornelius was either technically a pagan or at the very most a Jewish proselyte.

---

[22]Like the centurion, the Canaanite woman appears to have known nothing about Jesus except that he was a healer. Jesus praised the persistence and humility which she showed in her faith.

Notice the remarkable pattern here: a Christian (Peter) was learning religious truth from someone who had not yet received the gospel. And in the case of the exemplars whom Jesus commended, God's people were learning from those outside their traditions things that helped them better understand their own revelation. Jesus used pagans to teach his would-be disciples about faith, and Peter learned from a Gentile that Christ's mission extended to the Gentiles.

There is less evidence of this pattern in the Pauline writings. As one scholar has observed, Paul was schooled in the philosophical currents of his age but was not as concerned as other thinkers such as Philo (his contemporary, a Jewish philosopher) to reconcile his message with contemporary philosophy. He proclaimed that the gospel was the only means to divine wisdom (1 Cor 1:21; 2:6-16). While his writings resonate with certain Stoic and Cynic themes, there are profound differences on the nature of God and the human self. For Stoics, for example, self-sufficiency *(autarkēs)* comes from resolution of the will, while for Paul it springs from assurance of God's favor and presence. Cynic boldness was based on self-confidence and independence, but Paul's boldness was rooted in a sense of God's calling.[23]

On the other hand, it would be a mistake to conclude that Paul's thinking about God was not shaped in part by his cultural milieu—or, to put it more theologically—that God did not use Paul's cultural background and intellectual training to help shape his inspired insights. A distinguished scholar of the ancient world has observed that Paul and Epictetus sound remarkably similar at points because they both depended on a common tradition of (Stoic) rhetoric and reasoning. Paul in fact appropriated the style and commonplaces of his philosophical contemporaries; for example, he used the Stoic and Cynic traditions to describe his battles with his opponents at Corinth.[24] It is now a commonplace that the use of a tradition's symbols and reasoning to talk about God, self or world will shape the way one sees God, self and world. There can be little doubt, then, that God used Paul's culture to shape

---

[23]Terence P. Paige, "Philosophy," in *Dictionary of Paul and His Letters,* ed. Gerald F. Hawthorne and Ralph P. Martin (Downers Grove, Ill.: InterVarsity Press, 1993), pp. 713-18.

[24]Abraham J. Malherbe, *Paul and the Popular Philosophers* (Minneapolis: Fortress, 1989), esp. chaps. 2-3.

Paul's presentation of God's self-revelation. Therefore, while Paul was unique, he was also a man shaped by Hellenistic culture.[25] "After all, like Tennyson's Ulysses, and like the eclectic Plutarch or Musonius, we are part of all we have met. So was Paul."[26]

So we have solid evidence for the idea that the Bible portrays God's people as learning from people of other religions. Solid evidence, however, is not the same thing as proof. Most of the New Testament examples I have cited come from encounters with Jesus or preaching about Jesus. They are not examples of knowledge about God gained from sources completely disconnected from Jewish or Christian communities. Yet they nonetheless demonstrate that Jesus and Paul believed Christians could learn about God from individuals who knew little or nothing about Christ.

This chapter has shown us that the Bible is full of surprises on the religions. It shows that the God of the Bible wants people of other religions to know him, and that some of them have remarkable understanding of the true God. It also shows that his own people in Israel and the early church learned from people of other religions.

Now we are going to turn in the next two chapters to see even more surprising things about the Bible. We will see that both the Old (chap. 3) and the New (chap. 4) Testaments have a lot to say not only about other gods, but also about where they and the religions attached to them might have come from.

---

[25]Some might object that this is learning from culture and not religion. But as I explained in the introduction to this book, the line between religion and culture is very thin and sometimes nonexistent—much culture derives directly or indirectly from religious vision. And even if, in a given instance, culture is distinct from religion but Christians can learn truth from that culture, God is still teaching Christians truth through non-Christian means. The principle is the same.

[26]Malherbe, *Paul and the Popular Philosophers,* 9.

3

THE LORD OF HOSTS

The Old Testament and the
Real Existence of Other Gods

RELIGION IS A FUNNY THING. What is obvious to some is completely hidden from others. Take God's existence, for example. For strong believers, God's presence in all the world is evidenced in a thousand different ways, and the divine voice speaks all the time in innumerable ways. But for unbelievers, God seems nowhere. He appears to be silent.

This pattern of manifest presence to some and absence to others also applies to what believers see in the Bible. Some things that jump off the page for one generation of readers are almost invisible to another generation. It's a lot like figure 3.1, which was adapted from the German postcard on the left (1888) and the Anchor Buggy Company advertisement (1890).

Most of us see a pretty young woman. But if we are told there is also a wicked-looking old woman, suddenly, after a moment of concentration, we see her! We're astonished that she is also there. Unless someone had told us, we might never have seen the older woman. If not for help, the older woman might have forever remained invisible.

It's the same way for the existence of gods and spirits in the Bible. Most of us imagine the Bible teaches a simple monotheism in which there is one God, the physical cosmos, and nothing else "between"— except perhaps for angels.

The reality is profoundly different. Consider the following stories in the Bible. First is the story of Ahab's downfall, in which we see Yahweh consulting with supernatural beings called the "host of heaven" (הַשָּׁמַיִם צְבָא). Ahab was the king of Israel (ca. 875-854 B.C.E.) depicted by the

Figure 3.1.

Old Testament as the most evil of the ancient Jewish kings. It was his promotion of the worship of Baal that led to drought and famine and then to Elijah's eventual destruction of Baal's prophets (1 Kings 16:29—22:40). Just before the end of his life Ahab planned a war against Aram (modern Syria) and sought advice from his court prophets—four hundred in all. All but one prophesied success. Only Micaiah predicted disaster. In order to lend authority to his prediction, Micaiah described the circumstances in which he received his vision: he was an observer in Yahweh's heavenly court and overheard Yahweh discussing events with his supernatural advisers.

> Then Micaiah said, "Therefore hear the word of Yahweh: I saw Yahweh sitting on his throne, with all *the host of heaven standing beside him to the right and to the left of him.* And Yahweh said, 'Who will entice Ahab, so that he may go up and fall at Ramoth-gilead [a city east of the Jordan River that Ahab wanted to capture from Aram]?' Then *one said one thing, and another said another,* until *a spirit* came forward and stood before Yahweh, saying, 'I will entice him.' 'How?' Yahweh asked him. He replied, 'I will go out and be *a lying spirit* in the mouth of all his prophets.' Then Yahweh said, 'You are to entice him, and you shall succeed; go out and do it.' So you see, Yahweh has put *a lying spirit* in the mouth of all these your prophets; Yahweh has decreed disaster for you." (1 Kings 22:19-23, emphasis added)[1]

---

[1]As I have already stated, all translations unless otherwise noted are from the NRSV. However, I have replaced the NRSV's "the LORD" with "Yahweh" where the Hebrew permits. I do this in order to be more faithful to the text and also so the reader may be more attuned to the distinction that the text suggests between the God of Israel and the gods of the Gentiles.

Ahab went out to battle and was promptly killed by a stray arrow. "The dogs licked up his blood, and the prostitutes washed themselves in it" (1 Kings 22:38).

Did you notice what is often overlooked? The "host of heaven"—more helpfully translated "army of heaven"—consists of supernatural beings that have minds and wills of their own, apart from Yahweh's, and possess a degree of autonomy. In this case they assist Yahweh by doing what is necessary to fulfill Yahweh's goal: the destruction of Ahab. But for our topic the important—and intriguing—thing to notice is that there is a whole class of intermediate beings between the high God and his human creatures. Unless they are pointed out, they go unnoticed by most readers—just like the fierce-looking woman in the picture.

Consider another story. The prophet Daniel is standing on the bank of the Tigris river in Babylon in what is said to be "the third year of king Cyrus of Persia," which would make it 535 B.C.E. (most scholars think the book was written in the second century B.C.E., but the date is irrelevant to our concerns). He had seen a vision of "a great conflict" that presumably had the potential to harm his people, the Jews. So he had gone into mournful prayer for at least three weeks, fasting from meat, other rich food, wine and even fragrant oils. After three weeks of this fasting and prayer, an angel (probably Gabriel) appeared to him and told him that God's answer to his prayer had been held up because of opposition from another supernatural being, "the prince [מַלְכוּת, lit. "royal person"] of the kingdom of Persia" (Dan 10:13).

> [The angel] said to me, "Do not fear, Daniel, for from the first day that you set your mind to gain understanding and to humble yourself before your God, your words have been heard, and I have come because of your words. But the *prince of the kingdom of Persia* opposed me twenty-one days. So *Michael, one of the chief princes* [considered by Jews to be the chief angelic protector of the Jewish people], came to help me, and I left him there with the *prince of the kingdom of Persia,* and have come to help you understand what is to happen to your people at the end of days. For there is a further vision for those days. . . .
>
> [After strengthening Daniel, Gabriel continues:] Now I must return to fight against the *prince of Persia,* and when I am through with him, the *prince of Greece* will come. But I am to tell you what is inscribed in the

book of truth. There is no one with me who contends against *these princes* except *Michael, your prince*." (Dan 10:12-14, 20-21, emphasis added)

Once again there are supernatural beings, this time associated with royalty, with minds and wills of their own. This time some of them are actively opposed to Yahweh and his people, the Jews. The ones devoted to Yahweh's purposes, Michael and Gabriel, are thwarted in their attempts to carry out Yahweh's will by the opposition of the supernatural beings opposed to Yahweh and his people. Bottom line: Yahweh is not "alone" in the heavens, as it were. There are other supernatural beings "up there," some allied with him and working to carry out his designs, and others opposed to him and actively working to frustrate his purposes.

As if this were not surprising enough to the modern reader of the Bible, there's even more remarkable material in what Jews call *Tanakh* and Christians call the Old Testament: references to the gods. Many readers dismiss "gods" language as referring to empty idols, preferring to interpret "gods" as later chapters in Isaiah interpret them: "besides me there is no god" (Is 44:6). Later in this chapter I will argue that even this part of Isaiah may not be dismissing the reality of other gods. But at this point it is enough to say that most books of the Old Testament speak of "the gods" as existing realities—real spiritual beings with minds of their own.

Before we try to understand how these gods are related to Yahweh, let me first try to prove that they actually exist for most authors of the Old Testament.

The Psalms fairly explode with evidence. "There is none like you among the gods, O LORD" (Ps 86:8); "For great is the LORD, and greatly to be praised; he is to be revered above all gods" (Ps 96:4); "Our Lord is above all gods" (Ps 135:5); "Ascribe to Yahweh, [you] gods, ascribe to Yahweh glory and strength" (Ps 29:1, my trans.); "All gods bow down before him" (Ps 97:7); "For Yahweh is a great god, and a great king above all gods" (Ps 95:3, my trans.). And so on.

But it's not just the Psalms. In Exodus Yahweh predicts that he will execute judgments "on all the gods of Egypt" (Ex 12:12). The author of Numbers then declares that that is indeed what happened: "Yahweh executed judgments even against their gods" (Num 33:4). There is no hint that Yahweh is the only God. Instead it is clearly implied that Egypt has her own gods, and Yahweh will defeat them. When Yahweh gives his people the Ten Commandments, the first commandment implies the existence of other gods: "you shall have no other gods before me" (Ex 20:3; see also Deut 5:7). In Exodus 23:32-33 Israel is told not to covenant with or worship other gods; there is no suggestion that the gods of Israel's neighbors do not exist. Our thinking that the verse itself presumes the nonexistence of other gods owes more to our own prejudice than to the passage.[2]

Deuteronomy picks up this theme. Israel is told, "Do not follow other gods, any of the gods of the peoples who are all around you" (Deut 6:14). Yahweh predicts to Moses that after he dies, the Jewish tribes "will begin to prostitute themselves to the foreign gods in their midst, the gods of the land into which they are going" (Deut 31:16). Again, "the gods" seem to have real existence.

But Deuteronomy goes even further. It suggests that Yahweh had assigned other gods to the nations. When Moses warns the Israelites that they will be punished if they worship other gods, he predicts that "all the nations" will wonder why Yahweh's people "abandoned the covenant of the LORD, the God of their ancestors . . . and served other gods, worshiping them, gods whom they had not known *and whom he had not allotted to them*" (Deut 29:25-26, emphasis added). This allotment of gods to different peoples is cited just a few chapters later:

> When the Most High apportioned the nations,
> when he divided humankind,
> he fixed the boundaries of the peoples
> according to the number of *the gods;*
> Yahweh's own portion was his people,
> Jacob his allotted share. (Deut 32:8-9, emphasis added)

The implication is that Yahweh delegated supervision of other nations to other (in the context "subordinate") gods, while he exercised direct supervision of Israel. We will discuss this passage in greater detail later in this chapter.

Joshua and Judges continue to speak of Israel's departure from the

---

[2]For more on Western prejudice, see the famous article by Paul G. Hiebert, "The Flaw of the Excluded Middle," *Missiology* 10, no. 1 (January 1982): 35-47.

god of their ancestors to the gods of their neighbors (Josh 24:15; Judg 2:12; 6:10; 10:6) without a hint of the notion that the ancestors' gods are fictitious. Indeed, quite the opposite. In Judges 11 the Jewish leader Jephthah sends a message to the king of the Ammonites, who had made war on the Jews in order to get back territory the Jews had previously won in battle. Jephthah insists that Yahweh had won the disputed territory for his people. But he also assumes that the territory which the Ammonites currently possessed was won for them by their god Chemosh.

> So now Yahweh, the God of Israel, has conquered the Amorites [a general term for the entire aboriginal population of Canaan and therefore including the Ammonites] for the benefit of his people Israel. Do you intend to take their place? Should you not possess *what your god Chemosh gives you to possess?* And should we not be the ones to possess everything that Yahweh our God has conquered for our benefit? (Judg 11:23-24, emphasis added)

The most remarkable thing about this intriguing series of questions is not simply Jephthah's clear belief that Chemosh is real,[3] but his assumption (and presumably the assumption of the author/editor of Judges) that lands are won first and foremost by gods, and only secondarily by human forces. Furthermore, the text also assumes that each people or land has a different god assigned to it—which is what we saw in Deuteronomy.

Similar allusions to the reality of other gods can be found in most of the other historical books. In 1 Kings Solomon opens his prayer of dedication of his magnificent temple with the declaration, "O Yahweh, God of Israel, there is no God like you in heaven above or on earth beneath" (1 Kings 8:23). That Solomon believed in the other gods is clear, for the author chastises him for worshiping "Astarte the goddess of the Sidonians, Chemosh the god of Moab, and Milcom the god of the Ammonites" (1 Kings 11:33).

But even the author (or editor) of Kings seems to believe that these other gods existed. Ahab's son Ahaziah injured himself by falling and

---

[3]Many readers today think this was just Jephthah's way of making his case more compelling to the Ammonite king. But it is a scholarly consensus that Jephthah was assuming the reality of Chemosh. See, for example, Robert Goldenberg, *The Nations That Know Thee Not: Ancient Jewish Attitudes Toward Other Religions* (New York: New York University Press, 1998), p. 14.

sent messengers to ask of the Philistine god, Baal-zebub, whether he would recover. An angel of Yahweh told the prophet Elijah to meet the king's couriers with the message, "Is it because there is no god in Israel that you are going to inquire of Baal-zebub, the god of Ekron?" (2 Kings 1:3). Elijah's message was not that there are no other gods, but that the Jewish king ought to be seeking the God of the Jews, not the god of some other people.

This last story is not the strongest evidence because it is an argument from silence: Elijah does not assert the reality of Baal-zebub but simply fails to deny it. But there is stronger evidence in this same book of 2 Kings. It's the story of Israel's war with Moab, a people on the east shore of the Dead Sea. The kings of both Israel and Judah, along with the king of Edom, had attacked Moab with great success. All the Moabite cities but one had been overturned, and that last city was surrounded (2 Kings 3:21-25). But then, with his back against the wall, the king of Moab pulled out his ace in the hole, a card that only horrifies modern readers:

> he took his firstborn son who was to succeed him, and offered him as a burnt offering on the wall. And great wrath came upon Israel, so they withdrew from him and returned to their own land. (2 Kings 3:27)

Once we get over our revulsion for this king's barbarism, we must recognize the other remarkable feature of this story: the author clearly seems to believe that Moab's god was real, was pleased with this grisly sacrifice, and as a result did something that actually prevented Israel from completing its victory. The text does not tell us exactly what happened at this point, but it nevertheless makes plain that Chemosh (the god of Moab) liked the smell of the poor boy's flesh and rewarded his father's unfeeling ruthlessness by obstructing the Israelite army. In short, the gods are real and have genuine power to affect what happens on earth.

Thus, when we read the Old Testament with our eyes open to the possibility of other beings in the cosmos besides humans and Yahweh, we find some remarkable things. "The Old Testament speaks freely, without any hesitation or embarrassment, about the existence of gods other than the God of Israel. . . . To be sure, the supremacy of Israel's God over all other gods is everywhere asserted. But the assertion always drives home the dominion of Yahweh over other gods, not the denial of their existence."[4] This has been noted by a wide range of scholars, not only those primarily dedicated to university debate but also "conservative" scholars committed to orthodox and evangelical traditions.[5]

But now perhaps you have a question: If the gods have always been there in the Old Testament, why have so many generations of scholars and Bible readers not known this? Why have we not seen this before? There are several reasons. First, we see only what we think we're going to see. Since the Enlightenment, under the influence of deism, we have been trained to think of reality as either matter without spirit or matter and spirit without spirits. That is, those who have retained faith in supernatural reality have been accustomed to think that there are only God and us. Talk of "spirits" or "gods" is mythological and fanciful, the result of superstition.

Besides, we have been led to believe that the Bible teaches "pure" monotheism—God in heaven with only his angels and nothing else between them and us. The Old Testament, we have been taught, teaches that paganism is wrong because it is false. The pagan religions taught a multiplicity of gods, but the Hebrews, and particularly their eighth-century prophets, insisted that there is only one god, Yahweh, and that all others are empty idols. They don't exist and never did. So when we

---

[4]Ulrich Mauser, "One God Alone: A Pillar of Biblical Theology," *Princeton Seminary Bulletin* n.s. 12, no. 3 (1991): 259; quoted in Gregory A. Boyd, *God at War: The Bible & Spiritual Conflict* (Downers Grove, Ill.: InterVarsity Press, 1993), pp. 116-17.

[5]For a sampling of scholarship that has treated this phenomenon, see Mark S. Smith, *The Early History of God: Yahweh and the Other Deities in Ancient Israel* (San Francisco: Harper & Row, 1990); M. S. Smith, *The Origins of Biblical Monotheism: Israel's Polytheistic Background and the Ugaritic Texts* (New York: Oxford University Press, 2001); Goldenberg, *Nations That Know Thee Not*; E. Theodore Mullen Jr., *The Divine Council in Canaanite and Early Hebrew Literature* (Chico, Calif.: Scholars Press, 1980); John Day, *Yahweh and the Gods and Goddesses of Canaan* (Sheffield: Sheffield Academic Press, 2000); G. Ernest Wright, *The Old Testament Against Its Environment* (London: SCM Press, 1957); David Penchansky, *Twilight of the Gods: Polytheism in the Hebrew Bible* (Louisville, Ky.: Westminster John Knox, 2005); Penchansky, *What Rough Beast? Images of God in the Hebrew Bible* (Louisville, Ky.: Westminster John Knox, 1999); Bernhard Lang, "Wisdom," in *Dictionary of Deities and Demons in the Bible*, ed. Karel van der Toorn, 2nd ed. (Leiden: E.J. Brill, 1999), pp. 900-905; Peggy Lynn Day, "Satan in the Hebrew Bible" (Ph.D. diss., Harvard University, 1986).

For scholars who have identified themselves as committed to orthodox and/or evangelical traditions and have also noted this pattern, see N. T. Wright, *The New Testament and the People of God* (Minneapolis: Fortress, 1992), p. 258; Larry Hurtado, "First Century Jewish Monotheism," *Journal for the Study of the New Testament* 71 (1999): 3-26; Boyd, *God at War*, passim; Tremper Longman and Daniel G. Reid, *God Is a Warrior* (Grand Rapids: Zondervan, 1995), pp. 42, 64-65, 74-78, 81-82, 102, 142-53.

used to read the passages we have just seen in this chapter, we assumed the authors of the Bible were merely reporting what the pagans believed.

Or when we read "the Lord of hosts" we didn't stop to think what "hosts" could mean. If anything, we were told, it meant angels, not gods. And we knew that angels always did the will of God (except, of course, for Satan and his evil angels who have been known ever since as the devil and his demons). So "hosts" became simply extensions of God's own will and being. There simply didn't exist other supernatural beings with minds and wills that might oppose or even thwart Yahweh. Many Christians have even come to doubt the existence of Satan and demons as real entities.[6] So if we read about gods in Psalms, for instance, we assume it meant idols with no objective reality. In a sense, we never "saw" them, just as most of us never saw the old woman in the picture at the beginning of this chapter until someone showed us what to look for.

Translations were also a factor in what we saw or didn't see. We have already noted that Deuteronomy makes the remarkable assertion that Yahweh "fixed the boundaries of the peoples according to the number of the gods [literally, 'sons of gods'[7]]" (Deut 32:8-9). Until relatively recently, however, the established Hebrew text of the Old Testament (the Masoretic Text, produced between the third and eleventh centuries C.E.) read "according to the number of the sons of Israel" (based on the Masoretic *bene yisra'el*). But the discovery of the Dead Sea Scrolls in 1948, which contained fragments of Deuteronomy 32, has shown us that the proper reading is either *bene elohim* ("sons of the gods") or *bene 'el* ("sons of god").[8] This makes better sense of Deuteronomy 4:19 ("the host of heaven . . . whom Yahweh your God allotted . . . to all the peoples under heaven" [Mullen trans.]). It also helps explain why the Septuagint translation (the Greek version of the Old Testament that the early church relied on) of this passage reads "according to the number of the angels of God," and the apocryphal book of Sirach (or Ecclesiasticus, as it is also known) asserts, "For every nation he appointed a ruler, But Israel is the Lord's portion" (Sir 17:17). All these ver-

---

[6]As we will see in later chapters, New Testament authors and early church thinkers by and large came to see these "gods" as fallen angels.

[7]"Sons of gods" is a Hebrew idiom for beings with the same nature of gods—in other words, gods themselves.

[8]Mullen, *Divine Council*, pp. 202-3. Biblical quotations using Mullen's translation will be indicated in the parenthetical reference in the text.

sions and texts present a common picture: that God delegated rule of the nations to intermediate spiritual beings. But for centuries translations of the principal text, Deuteronomy 32:8-9, followed what was probably a later and therefore corrupted reading. Because the Masoretic Text followed manuscripts that were later and not original, it helped blind Bible readers to the Bible's vision of a cosmos full of gods and spirits.

A final reason for our inability to see the gods of the Old Testament is the "pure" monotheism that prophets like Isaiah seem to proclaim. As Isaiah asks, "Is there any god besides me? There is no other rock; I know not one" (Is 44:8). This apparently pure monotheism seems for many of us to overwhelm all evidence of any other Hebrew beliefs. Either we assume this is what other biblical authors really meant, or we think this represents the apogee of development in biblical theology—that over time God led the Jews from belief in gods under Yahweh to, eventually, recognition that other gods do not exist.

The problem with letting such a statement from Isaiah represent mainstream Old Testament belief—as either its inner or culminating meaning—is that the book of Isaiah itself contains counterevidence. In chapter six Yahweh is presented as having a council with which he consults (Is 6:2-8). And the same Second Isaiah[9] who seems to teach the unreality of the gods likewise suggests that nations, princes and armies are as nothing before Yahweh (Is 40:17, 23; 41:12). For example, "All the nations are as nothing before him; they are accounted by him as less than nothing and emptiness" (Is 40:17). Perhaps such language, both for other rulers and the gods, is literary hyperbole with a point: the nations and the gods, compared to Yahweh, are nothing.

But even if Second Isaiah really denies the objective reality of the gods, this would not solve the problem. Most other Old Testament authors still assert or suggest their existence. Right alongside texts that (might) deny any other gods but Yahweh are texts that acknowledge them. This cannot be denied. So if we assert that there is evidence for "pure" monotheism in the Old Testament, we also have to say that there is in fact more evidence for what N. T. Wright calls "creational monotheism," which means that Yahweh rules over a cosmos inhabited by other

---

[9]The name given by many scholars for the author or editor of most or all of chapters 40—66.

supernatural beings as well as human, angelic and animal creatures. In the ancient world, "we have very few examples of 'pure' monotheism anywhere, including in the Hebrew Bible."[10]

In the rest of this chapter we shall look at what is called the "divine council," which is the most common way the Old Testament pictures these gods/supernatural beings.[11] We will see what functions the gods perform and then see how the Old Testament view of these gods varies, or perhaps progresses, over time. We will ask how this compares to the pagan religions of the ancient Near East, and then finally reflect on what this means for Old Testament views of other religions. The upshot of all this is that, contrary to what many would now imagine, the Old Testament has plenty to say about other religions. And what it has to say is quite different from what most of us would have predicted.

The Divine Council

The most common way in which the gods are pictured in the Old Testament is as members of what is called the "divine council." This is an assembly of lesser supernatural figures, subordinated to Yahweh for his consultation and direction. Mark S. Smith calls it (in its later forms) a "streamlined bureaucracy headed by an absolute monarch."[12]

Psalm 89:5-8 paints the picture with clear strokes:

> The heavens praise your wonders, O Yahweh,
> And your truth in *the council* of the holy ones.[13]
> For who in the skies can compare to Yahweh?
> Who is like Yahweh among the sons of god (i.e., the gods)?
> A dreadful god in *the council* of the holy ones,
> Great and terrible above all those around him.
> Yahweh, god of (the heavenly) hosts, who is like you?
> Mighty Yah(weh), your faithful ones surround you. (Mullen trans., p. 191)

---

[10]Wright, *New Testament and the People of God*, p. 258.

[11]Some readers will think these are very different things, since a God must be a creator of the cosmos, while even a minor angel without creative power can be a "divine being." Yet, as we have begun to see, the OT uses the word *elohim* ("gods") for beings that are separate from Yahweh, who alone is called Creator; see, for example, Ps 95:3 and Ps 104:1-9. For many OT authors, then, there are "gods," but there is only one God who created the world.

[12]M. S. Smith, *Origins of Biblical Monotheism*, p. 78.

[13]In the OT, "holy" does not have the same meaning as our English word: rather than necessarily emphasizing purity and sinlessness, it denotes being set apart and separate.

Sometimes the gods in the divine council are represented as the "the holy ones," as in Zechariah and Job. Zechariah predicts that on the Day of the Lord (the decisive visitation by Yahweh to earth when he would vindicate Israel over against her enemies), "Yahweh my God will come, and all the holy ones with him" (Zech 14:5). Job asserts that Yahweh "puts no trust even in his holy ones" (Job 15:15). At other times they are referred to as the heavenly host or army of Yahweh.

But there is little question that no matter what the members of the council are called, they are represented as being inferior to Yahweh. The psalmist says Yahweh is "feared in the council of the holy ones" (Ps 89:7), and declares that "all gods bow down before him" (Ps 97:7). "I know that Yahweh is great; our Lord is above all gods" (Ps 135:5). Moses asks, "Who is like you among the gods, O Yahweh? Who is like you, terrible among the holy ones?" (Ex 15:11, Mullen trans.) Yahweh's preeminence over all other heavenly beings can be seen throughout the Old Testament (see also, for example, Deut 10:17; 1 Kings 8:23; 1 Chron 16:25; Ps 86:8; 95:3; 96:4; 136:2).

The members of the divine council have various functions. First and foremost is service. Although we have already seen that some supernatural beings thwarted Yahweh's will, it is clear that they were intended, and presumably created, to serve Yahweh's larger agenda. The "host of heaven" in the 1 Kings 22 story about Ahab and Micaiah were at Yahweh's beck and call, eager to assist Yahweh in his determination to destroy Ahab. The seraphim in Yahweh's throne room in Isaiah 6 are dedicated to his glory and service. It is interesting that the basic structure of the scene is the same as in 1 Kings 22: Yahweh is on his throne, before him are supernatural beings, and he asks who will perform a mission for him. The only difference is that while in 1 Kings it is a spirit that volunteers, in Isaiah it is the prophet himself. But in both cases Yahweh responds with an emphatic "Go!" Supernatural beings are there to serve Yahweh's purposes, to carry out his decisions.

Mullen's translation of Deuteronomy 33:2-3 presents a vivid illustration:

With him were myriads of holy ones,
At his right hand marched the mighty ones,
Yea the guardians of the people.
All the holy ones are at your right hand.

They prostrate themselves at your feet,
They carry out your decisions. (Mullen trans., emphasis added)

The scene in Isaiah 6 demonstrates another function of the supernatural beings in Yahweh's council: worship. They also exist as instruments of praise. The seraphim cry out, "Holy, holy, holy is Yahweh of hosts; the whole earth is full of his glory" (Is 6:3). Second Isaiah states that Yahweh brings out, numbers and knows by name the sun, moon and stars (who were thought in the ancient Near East to be divine beings) (Is 40:26). The Deuteronomic editor commands, "Worship him, all you gods!" (Deut 32:43) The psalmist says the same:

Ascribe to Yahweh, O gods!
Ascribe to Yahweh glory and honor!
Ascribe to Yahweh the glory of his name!
Prostrate yourselves to Yahweh when he appears in holiness! (Ps 29:1-2, Mullen trans.)

The gods are also supposed to accompany Yahweh in warfare. The psalmist proclaims,

The chariots of God are two thousand;
Thousands are the warriors/archers of Yahweh
When he came from Sinai with the holy ones. (Ps 68:17, Mullen trans.)

The same theme is taken up by the author/editor of Judges, who seems to regard the stars as supernatural powers enlisted by Yahweh to go with him to battle: "From the heavens the stars fought, from their stations they fought with Sisera [commander of the Canaanite forces defeated by Israel under the leadership of Barak and Deborah]" (Judg 5:20, Mullen trans.).[14]

We have already seen from our look at Daniel 10 that another function of at least some of these supernatural beings was to rule the nations. We saw that the original text of Deuteronomy 32:8-9 says that Yahweh established "the boundaries of the peoples according to the number of the gods," and that Yahweh kept "Jacob" (another name for Israel) for himself to rule directly. In Deuteronomy 4:19 the Israelites

---

[14]Some Jews apparently interpreted these stars as national angels who were opposed to Yahweh. See n. 10 in chap. 4.

are forbidden from worshiping "the sun, the moon, and the stars, all the host of heaven . . . [which] Yahweh your god has allotted to all the peoples everywhere under heaven." In other words, they were told not to worship other gods, not because those gods did not exist, but because they were supposed to rule other peoples, not Israel. Yahweh himself, who created and rules the other gods, would rule Israel directly. He would rule the nations indirectly through the delegated authority of the gods appointed. This, apparently, was the original intent behind the strange authority that the "prince of Persia" possessed in Daniel 10. He was then thwarting Yahweh's will, but originally he was intended to rule Persia *for* Yahweh.

Something had gone terribly wrong. But Yahweh was not going to let the matter stand. Psalm 82 is a startling depiction of Yahweh's forthright action to correct the problem. The supernatural beings he had appointed to rule the nations justly had failed to perform. They were supposed to rule with justice, executing judgments on behalf of the poor, the widows and the rest of the nations. But because they did not judge properly, Yahweh would judge them. And the punishment is ferocious:

[Yahweh] has taken his place in *the divine council,*
In the midst of the *gods* he passes judgment.
"How long will you judge unjustly, and exalt the case of the wicked?
Vindicate the poor and the orphan,
Maintain the justice of the afflicted and the needy!
Deliver the weak and the poor,
Rescue them from the power of the wicked!"
They neither know nor understand.
They wander about in darkness,
All the foundations of the earth are shaken.
I had thought, "*You are gods,*
And all of you, sons of Elyon [God Most High]."
Instead *like Adam you shall die,*
And like one of the "Shining Ones" you shall fall.

"Arise, O Yahweh; Judge the earth!
May you take possession of all the nations!"
(Ps 82, Mullen trans.)

Notice the intriguing statements and suggestions in this psalm. The gods' function, among other things, was to rule their nations with justice, which meant caring for the poor and afflicted. Since they failed to perform their assigned function, Yahweh condemned them to death. In the last two verses the psalmist calls on Yahweh to "judge the earth" and "take possession of all the earth," which probably means to take back control of the nations from the gods, who have abused their authority.

There is a hint in verse 7 of rebellion against Yahweh. It calls to mind Isaiah 14 and Ezekiel 28, where the king of Babylon and prince of Tyre are condemned for their rebellious pride. In Isaiah 14:12-14, the rebellion is explicit. The "Shining One, son of Dawn" (notice the same phrase used here in Ps 82:7) tried to place himself above "the stars of El [the highest God, or Yahweh]" to "sit enthroned in the Mount of Assembly (of the gods)," to "be like Elyon [the fuller name for the Most High God]" (Mullen trans.).

The drift of these passages is that the gods are condemned to death not simply because of their failure to rule with justice, but more importantly, for their rebellion against their maker, Yahweh. Their unjust rule of the nations was simply one of many expressions of their rebellion, which was the principal reason for Yahweh's discipline. Later, as we shall see, Christians came to see these two stories in the prophets as allusions to Satan's fall from grace. Once created as God's most gifted and beautiful supernatural being, Satan abused his authority and then led a rebellion against Yahweh. God punished him by limiting his authority on earth; he is still the "god of this world" (2 Cor 4:4), but his authority is checked by God's sovereign purposes, and his final destruction is decreed.

If the gods were to rule the nations with justice, they were also supposed to carry out God's judgments against the wicked. This is what the members of the divine council in fact did in 1 Kings 22—they executed God's judgment against wicked Ahab by enticing Ahab to march into a battle where Yahweh had, as it were, prepared an ambush for him. When Yahweh, in the midst of his divine assembly in Isaiah 6, sends out the prophet, it is to pronounce judgment on Israel: "Make the mind of this people dull, and stop their ears . . . until cities lie waste without inhabitant, and houses without people, and the land is utterly desolate" (Is 6:10-11). And the supernatural being called the "messenger of Yahweh" in Judges 5 is sent to "curse Meroz [a town in the Jezreel valley] . . . curse bitterly its inhabitants, because they did not come to the help of Yahweh, to the help of Yahweh against the mighty" (Judg 5:23).

Let's take a moment to recall what we have seen: The gods in the divine council are typically portrayed by the Old Testament as inferior beings subordinated to him. They were appointed by Yahweh as his servants to praise him, accompany him in battle, execute his wrath against the wicked and rule the nations with justice. Because they failed to do the latter, they were punished with death—though the nature of that death is not specified.

Is There a Progression in Thinking About the Gods?

I just said this is the typical way the gods are portrayed—as members of a council dedicated to serving Yahweh. But the traces of the gods and other supernatural beings in the Old Testament is not that simple or clean. They are pictured in other ways and with other names, as we have already observed. There are angels and spirits and seraphim and gods and the Most High God—and others. Not to mention Yahweh. How are they all related? Since we know that the Old Testament books were written at different times and that some of these books were probably edited compilations and revisions of earlier documents, do these different words and entities represent different stages in Jewish thinking about the heavens? Can we trace an evolution in thinking? Is there any sort of progression?

Scholars have suggested different answers to these questions. Most recent scholars believe there has been an evolution of belief. If not an orderly progression, at the very least there are different views placed alongside one another. It is not worth our time to detail all of these theories or speculate which is the most plausible. But for simplicity and curiosity sake, I will briefly explain an understanding of this variety that incorporates what could be called a composite view of the majority of scholarly opinion on this question.

In the first period, running from the twelfth century B.C.E. down to just before the Babylonian exile, texts were written portraying the divine council over which Yahweh presides. The subordinate gods in this council suggest strategy to Yahweh, praise Yahweh and administer other nations for Yahweh. This phase is particularly evident in the reference to

Yahweh as "God of gods" that we see in the Psalms and elsewhere. God is the "Lord of hosts" whose name suggests that he created the gods: "Yahweh Elohim," typically translated as "the LORD God," may mean "He who summons the gods into being."[15] During this period the other gods might have been viewed as worthy of honor and respect, just as any earthly king's subordinates would be worthy of honor and respect.

But then reaction set in. The idea that other deities may be honored, which is never stated explicitly but seems to lie under the surface of some biblical texts, is vehemently rejected. Thus in Psalm 82 an angry Yahweh rebukes the gods for dereliction of duty. Worship or even honor of other deities becomes unthinkable. This period is thought to have begun in the ninth century B.C.E., after reflection on Solomon's idolatrous shrines to Yahweh's subordinates—Astarte, Milkom and Chemosh (1 Kings 11:5-7; 2 Kings 23:13-14)—and Ahab's installation of a new temple in Samaria. It reaches its sharpest expression in Deuteronomy 13:6-11, where Israelites are told to report on family members who worship other gods.

Finally, during and after the Babylonian exile (6th century B.C.E.), comes the consideration that, at least in relation to Yahweh, the other gods are no gods at all. Second Isaiah mocks the pagans who make their gods out of wood (Is 44:9-17), and Jeremiah treats pagan deities as "no-gods" (Jer 2:11; 5:7; 16:20).

Are these "stages" (if they were stages at all, and not simply competing visions) in conflict? Do they mean that the Old Testament presents contradictory views of God and the gods? That the lesser gods both exist and do not exist? Both that they can be honored and that even consideration of that is idolatrous?

The short answer to these questions is that conflict between portraits of God (and his relation to anything else, including other entities—human or supernatural) does not necessarily mean contradiction. The history of Christian thinking has always wrestled with apparent antinomies. One example has been the apparent contradiction between God's love and wrath. Another has been the apparent conflict between his control of all things (usually called his sovereignty) and human freedom. Still an-

---

[15]Baruch Halpern, "Monotheism," in *The Oxford Companion to the Bible,* ed. Bruce M. Metzger and Michael D. Coogan (New York: Oxford University Press, 1993), p. 525.

other, which was pretty much settled after "only" three centuries, was
the apparent conflict between the notions that God is one and God is
also somehow three. Most Christian theologians have taken a "compati-
bilist" approach to these and many other supposed contradictions—that
they can be reconciled without being irrational. Most theologians also
believe those differing perspectives contribute to a vision of God that,
while not being simple and without difficulty, is nevertheless without
absurd contradictions.

Christian theology has also recognized for thousands of years that revelation has been progressive, which means that the picture of God
evolves through the Bible. Some things are shown in the New Testament
that are not shown so clearly in the Old. And some concepts seem to
develop in stages, as it were, through the Old Testament.

So the idea that the relation of God to the gods in the Old Testament
changes from passage to passage or book to book should not be trou-
bling to Christian understanding. The trick is to figure out how to understand this development or series of contrasting images. We will see in
the next chapter, for example, that the early church resolved these questions by seeing these "gods" as demons and cosmic powers that war with
Christ and his kingdom.

Is This Pagan?

But in the meantime, doesn't a lot of this seem awfully pagan? Especially
talk about a divine council with Yahweh consulting with other supernatural beings?

Not when you consider the immense differences between pagan and
biblical cosmology (view of the cosmos or what we would call ultimate
reality). First of all, among Israel's pagan neighbors, the gods were
roughly comparable in stature and power so that there were many rival-
ries and assorted relations (often sexual) among them. But for Israel,
Yahweh brooked no rivals. There was only a single council of the ruler
and the ruled. There were no other relations among the gods. Furthermore, Yahweh had no consort, no sexual partner, no children conceived
by sexual acts. The Old Testament rejected the Canaanite symbolism of
El (its god) as a bull and Asherah as his wife. The Bible shifted the paradigm "from the model of the divine couple in charge of the four-tiered

pantheon to a single figure surrounded by minor powers, who are only expressions of that divinity's power."[16]

Second, while for ancient Near Eastern pagans, monsters and gods challenge the high god for mastery, Yahweh is depicted in the Old Testament as having conquered them all. Some still challenge, but there is no doubt that in future fights Yahweh will win again. The monsters are subservient to Yahweh in Psalm 148:7 ("Praise Yahweh from the earth, you sea monsters and all deeps"), Leviathan is a "tamed pet" in Job 41 and Psalm 104:26,[17] and in Genesis 1 the cosmic forces are no longer divine—as they were for many of Israel's pagan neighbors.

Finally, the Israelites believed there was only one true God. There were other "gods," but none had the power of Yahweh, and they were probably created by Yahweh anyway. What power they have is on loan from Yahweh. In fact, as some Old Testament texts proclaim, Yahweh alone is the creator of all. He alone is therefore sovereign of all. And he alone is eternal.

So while there are some superficial similarities to pagan religions of the ancient Near East—in that both Israel and her neighbors believe in a cosmos animated by a variety of powers—they still display significant differences. And there are enough differences to sharply distinguish biblical religion from pagan religion.

Summing Up: Yahweh and the Gods

What can we say about the Old Testament and the religions? As we have seen, there are generally four approaches taken in this collection of books. First, there is what one scholar has called "neighborly pluralism."[18] This is the attitude that other peoples have their own gods, which Yahweh has assigned to them. The other gods are subordinated to Yahweh and probably created by him. As long as they leave us Jews alone to worship Yahweh, we can leave them alone. Jephthah assumes the Ammonites can get along with their god Chemosh and their land so long as Israel is permitted to keep its religion and land. This attitude lies behind the Daniel 10 passage we saw above (only there the god of Persia

---

[16]M. S. Smith, *Origins of Biblical Monotheism*, p. 47.
[17]Ibid., p. 36.
[18]Goldenberg, *Nations That Know Thee Not*, p. 10.

was now resisting Yahweh), and it certainly lies behind Micah 4:5: "For all the peoples walk, each in the name of its god, but we will walk in the name of the LORD our God forever and ever." It probably also inspires the author of Jonah, who in the first chapter presents the sailors each calling on the name of his own god to protect the ship. Jonah told them that Yahweh made the sea (and so is greater than their gods who seem more localized), but there is no hint of hostility toward their gods and religions (Jon 1:5-14).

The second view is "competitive pluralism."[19] This roughly corresponds to the second period I outlined a few pages back, in which it is decided there is absolutely no room for honor or worship to be given to other gods—even if they were originally created as part of a divine council. Moses, for example, denied there was any like Yahweh among the gods, and his father-in-law Jethro, a pagan, says the same (Ex 15:11; 18:11). This is the attitude we saw in Psalm 82, which is an angry dismissal of foreign deities as once divine but now demoted. We also see this perspective in Elijah's triumphant declaration after "defeating" the prophets of Baal on Mt. Carmel: "Yahweh is the gods! Yahweh is the gods!" (1 Kings 18:39, my trans.) In other words, no other god has Yahweh's power.

There is also "vehement missionary exclusivism."[20] This is the explicit denial of the reality of other gods. This attitude says there is indeed only one god, and his name is Yahweh. All other gods are figments of the imagination of non-Jews. Yahweh alone is in the heavens. No other supernatural powers exist, except perhaps for Yahweh's angels. As I argued earlier in this chapter, it is not clear that any Old Testament author holds this view—even Second Isaiah, who seems its chief proponent. In that case, he was the chief representative of a missionary exclusivism that not only wants to tell the nations that they should convert to Yahwehism, but also that their gods and religions are, if not nonexistent, at least imperfect and misleading.

But there is still another view, not necessarily in complete distinction from all of the preceding, but different enough in emphasis that we must

---

[19]Ibid.
[20]Ibid.

discuss it. This is the "cosmic war" view. It rejects the "Yahweh alone" view that denies the existence of any other gods. It might refuse to call them "gods," but when it does that it is only quibbling with words. For it believes the cosmos is full of supernatural powers and that they are fully engaged with Yahweh and his plans.

There are traces here of the Canaanite and Mesopotamian religious myths of Tiamat, Yamm and Leviathan—stories about rival gods that are embodied in nature and fight for control of the cosmos. The Old Testament makes clear that the cosmic forces that these deities represented were defeated by Yahweh, but at the same time the Bible suggests the war is ongoing. For example, Yahweh defeated the sea (which represented the power of Yamm for the Canaanites) in Job 38:6-11; Psalms 29:3-4, 10; 104:6-9. But the psalmist still prays for deliverance from the deep (Ps 69:14-15). By the same token, Yahweh has crushed Leviathan (another Canaanite monster representing primal cosmic power) in Psalm 74:14, and yet Yahweh will continue to defeat him (Is 27:1).[21]

The point of these allusions scattered throughout the Old Testament seems to be that while the pagan stories of these powers are largely false, they are also partly true. The truth is that the cosmos is still at war and there are supernatural beings other than Yahweh. Yahweh has defeated these hostile powers, but the war is ongoing. This is a bit like D-day, the sixtieth anniversary of which we celebrated in 2004. That gigantic battle broke the back of the Wehrmacht, and so for the most part won World War II. But there was still to be almost another year of war in Europe, with many more bloody battles and much loss of life. Like D-day, Yahweh's primal victories over these hostile powers were decisive, but battles still continue to be waged to reinforce and reaffirm those first, decisive conquests.

What about the religions? At one level, the answer is not very difficult. The Old Testament takes these four approaches to Gentile religions. The first is neighborly pluralism: other religions are led by real gods but gods subordinate to ours; we can get along as long as they leave us alone. We

---

[21]See Jon D. Levenson, *Creation and the Persistence of Evil: The Jewish Drama of Divine Omnipotence* (San Francisco: Harper & Row, 1998).

might even honor their gods to the extent they are worthy of honor.

The second is competitive pluralism: other religions are not worthy of honor because at their head are deities that rebelled against Yahweh and violated his contract with them. Rather than fulfilling the functions to which they had been assigned—to administer the nations as delegated servants of Yahweh—they enticed their charges to give exclusive devotion to themselves. The Hebrew prophets said this is in fact what the Israelites themselves had done, giving idolatrous devotion to lesser powers, instead of exclusive devotion to Yahweh. So according to this view, the Gentile religions were cults devoted to real but treasonous powers.

The third model is vehement missionary exclusivism: other religions are devotion to what are not gods. Or if their gods have any existence, they are weak and pathetic, infinitely inferior to the only creator, Yahweh.

The fourth model, cosmic war, sees the religions as communities animated by powers hostile to Yahweh, actively fighting Yahweh's control of the cosmos. It is no surprise that history is full of conflict because its driving animus is conflict between supernatural forces, which are visibly represented by both religious and political communities. In other words, wars between nations are really only the shadowy surface of the deeper and more fundamental combat between spiritual powers. So Samuel Huntington, the Harvard political scientist whose *Clash of Civilizations* (1996) claimed that the real inspiration for modern war will be cultural and religious, was representing what could be called one Old Testament model.[22]

So there you have the easy answer to the question of what the Old Testament says about other religions. It presents these four models, and they are not mutually exclusive. In fact, they are often complementary; missionary exclusivism and competitive pluralism often exist in tandem with the cosmic war view.

The difficult part of the question is figuring out how to use these mod-

---

[22]Huntington, of course, makes no claim to a supernatural dimension in geopolitics (*Clash of Civilizations* [New York: Simon & Schuster, 1996]). And while he portrays a clash between Western and non-Western powers, both groups of which are associated with world religions, I make no claim that Christianity is associated with the West. In fact, Christianity is now more common in the global South than the developed West. But I still hold that there is a parallel between the biblical view of spiritual forces animating national concerns and Huntington's thesis that religion and culture underlie major civilizations.

els for today, or if and how they could be compatible—particularly for historic Christians who have always insisted that the Bible, despite its many authors, has a single Author who was superintending its writing to present a single—if differentiated—vision. The best way to handle this difficult task is to look at how Christian thinkers approached it in the next few centuries. Which is what we shall do. But in the meantime, we will first explore how the New Testament developed this thinking about the religions in new ways.

4

PRINCIPALITIES AND POWERS

The New Testament on Other
Real Supernatural Powers Besides God

IN 55 C.E. THE APOSTLE PAUL HAD A SERIOUS PROBLEM. The church he had helped start in Corinth ("the New York, Los Angeles and Las Vegas of the ancient world"[1]) was torn over the question of idolatry.

Corinth, like any Greek city in the first century, was dotted with pagan temples dedicated to various deities. These temples held regular services that featured sacrifices of meat to a deity. After the sacrificial offering, part of the meat was consumed at an open feast dedicated to the god, and other parts of the meat were sold in the marketplace. The feast dedicated to a god was a common feature of city life in Greek cities, and it served as a restaurant for people wanting to dine out. Most Greeks believed that the god was a guest at these feasts and in fact entered into the bodies and spirits of the eaters through the meat.

The question that bedeviled the Christian church at Corinth was, Can a Christian dine at these pagan restaurants? Or, Can a Christian buy and eat this meat, originally dedicated to a god, in the marketplace?

Greek Christians, who had grown up eating at such restaurants all their lives before conversion, tended to say, "Why not? We know there is only one god, the Father of Jesus Christ. Therefore these pagan gods don't exist. What doesn't exist can't hurt you. Eating this meat either in

---

[1]Gordon Fee, *The First Epistle to the Corinthians* (Grand Rapids: Eerdmans, 1987), p. 3. By this Fee meant that first-century Corinth was extremely diverse religiously, and that because of its wealth attracted not only artisans and tradesmen but also artists, philosophers, itinerants and charlatans of all kinds.

public or at home proves our freedom in Christ." Jewish Christians, on
the other hand, who had grown up with Jewish rules against touching
such "idolatrous" meat, believed that eating dedicated meat was anath-
ema no matter where it was consumed.

This difference of opinion led to problems. "Weak" believers (usually
Jews who had recently accepted Jesus as Messiah) were deeply troubled
by seeing fellow believers (usually Greeks who saw Jesus as the cosmic
Lord) eat "pagan" meat without compunction. Some of these "weak" believers were losing their faith as a result. As Paul put it to the "strong,"
"The weak brother, for whom Christ died, is destroyed by your knowledge" (1 Cor 8:11 NIV).

The other problem was that the "strong" believers, who imagined
their knowledge (that other gods do not exist) kept them safe, were in
reality (Paul believed) consorting with demons. Their "pure" monotheism (recall the last chapter) was ironically opening them up to infection
by malevolent powers. Paul said they were dining with demons and pro-
voking the Lord to jealousy (1 Cor 10:21-22).

This question about meat offered to idols was one of the reasons Paul
wrote 1 Corinthians. In this letter he addressed both the weak and the
strong. To the weak Paul said that since God made all things, meat in
itself cannot hurt a Christian believer. Even if dining in the house of a
pagan, a Christian can eat such meat without question (1 Cor 10:25-27).

But to the strong Paul said they were playing with fire. Yes, the gods
do not exist. But the *powers* do! Lurking behind the nonexistent gods
were evil spiritual forces, seducing humans away from worship of the
true God (1 Cor 10:18-22). Besides, Paul suggested, you are hurting others who observe you. To paraphrase the message of 1 Corinthians
10:27—11:1, "So even if eating idol meat is harmless for you," Paul said
to the strong, "it can hurt those without your knowledge. So if you know
they are threatened by your practice, you must give up your practice.
Love, not just knowledge, should govern your behavior."

Paul told his church at Corinth that in their own homes they could eat
meat bought in the marketplace. Even if it had been once dedicated to
a deity, they knew that no food is unclean to a believer who gives thanks
for it to God (1 Cor 10:25-26; cf. 1 Tim 4:3-5). But the new Christian rule
was love, which meant consideration of how one's actions would affect

others. If eating something would cause a brother or sister to stumble, one should not eat that.

A second new rule was, Do not participate in pagan feasts at their temples. Such participation is really participation in demonic realities in and behind pagan idolatry.

As we can see from this crisis in the little Christian church in Corinth, Paul believed in other spiritual beings beyond the God of Israel and Father of Jesus Christ. He told the Corinthian Christians quite directly, in fact, "There are many gods and many lords" (1 Cor 8:5). Significantly, Paul used the same titles—god and lord—which he and all Jews used for the one true God. He was no innovator when he said this. Jewish tradition already held that pagan sacrifices were made to spiritual powers hostile to Yahweh. The author of Deuteronomy had written that when ancient Israelites had worshiped pagan deities, they "sacrificed to demons that were no gods" (Deut 32:17).[2] The psalmist had written that when, in imitation of their pagan neighbors, Jews had offered their own children as sacrifices, "they sacrificed their sons and their daughters to the demons" (Ps 106:37).

For Jews, demons were not gods on par with Yahweh. Yahweh was the only Creator and Lord of the cosmos. Instead, the pagan gods were angelic or some other kind of spiritual beings, who stood behind the nations and their religions. We saw this in the last chapter.

We shall see in this chapter that Paul's understanding was similar. In fact, the "principalities and powers" (language used by Paul to describe these forces) were fundamental to his view of the world. "The idea of sinister world powers and their subjugation by Christ is built into the very fabric of Paul's thought, and some mention of them is found in every epistle except Philemon."[3] Paul's belief that the powers are the invisible agents behind what really happens in the world is especially seen in Ephesians 6:12:

Our struggle is not against enemies of blood and flesh, but against the rul-

---

[2]This is in the same chapter that speaks of Yahweh's apportioning the nations to the "sons of the gods" (Deut 32:8). These seem to be different kinds of beings, for they are called demons—*sed'im*—which appear to be the plural of the Akkadian minor deity *sedu*.

[3]George Bradford Caird, *Principalities and Powers: A Study in Pauline Theology* (Oxford: Clarendon, 1956), p. vii.

ers, against the authorities, against the cosmic powers of this present darkness, against the spiritual forces of evil in the heavenly places.[4]

In other words, behind much human opposition to God's work in the world are invisible spiritual powers. We miss the real enemy when we direct our attacks against human beings.

But before we unpack the meaning of all this, let's look at how these ideas fit into the more general religious context of the first-century Mediterranean world. Paul's view of the powers, which to most of us is quite strange, will be a little more plausible when seen against its Hellenistic and Jewish background.

The Hellenistic Context

Plato had taught that the stars are "visible and created gods" that derive their divinity from the one God, the Demiurge.[5] He wrote that cities and other parts of the cosmos are ruled by spiritual powers which have been given specific spheres of authority.[6] Aristotle taught something similar.[7]

In popular Roman religion, it was commonly believed that a supreme divine power (called the Logos or Providence) was in charge of all things, and had delegated authority to various subordinate spiritual beings. Therefore no educated person in the Roman empire of the first century (this was the Hellenistic world, so-named because Greek culture was pervasive) would have been surprised by a new religion that reduced the Greco-Roman gods to powers *(dynameis)* under the authority of a supreme God. Besides, astrology, which was also common currency, had taught the first-century mind that one's daily life is controlled largely by astral influences.

The Jewish Background

As we have seen from the last chapter and our brief look at Corinth above, Jews had similar conceptions. Like the Greeks, some Jews be-

---

[4]Scholars disagree on whether Ephesians and Colossians are genuinely Pauline. In this essay, I will assume what even many of the "anti-genuine" scholars assume: that if they were not penned by the apostle himself, they were composed by someone in a school infused with the apostle's thinking. For that reason, I will treat them as representing "Paul."

[5]*Timaeus* 40a, 40c, 40d, 41a.

[6]*Laws* 4.713c-e; 5.738d; 10.903b.

[7]*On the Heavens* 292b.

lieved in delegated spiritual powers linked to the stars. In *1 Enoch,* a popular apocryphal work written in the first century, an angel named Uriel is associated with the stars. More explicit is *The Testament of Solomon,* a Jewish-Christian work usually dated in the third century C.E. but possibly containing material from the first century. This document straightforwardly speaks of star spirits called *stoicheia:*[8] "We are the *stoicheia,* rulers of this world of darkness. . . . Our stars in heaven look small, but we are named like gods" (*Testament of Solomon* 8:2-4).

Most Hellenistic Jews accommodated these Greek astral deities to their own cosmology, which envisioned not gods in their own right but angelic viceroys with delegated powers. They saw the powers in terms of Daniel 10, where the nations have angels who were originally created and commissioned by Yahweh, but have since fallen and are now hostile to Yahweh. We see this belief reflected in the book of *Jubilees* (2nd century B.C.E.):

> The Lord sanctified [Israel] and gathered [them] from all mankind. For there are many nations and many peoples and all belong to him. He made *spirits* rule over all in order to lead them astray from following him. But over Israel he made no *angel* or *spirit* rule because he alone is their ruler. (*Jubilees* 15:31-32; emphasis added)

We see another reflection of this worldview in Philo, the great Jewish thinker who was a contemporary of the apostle Paul. Philo believed that the supreme God providentially governs the cosmos through intermediate powers, some of which are responsible for the government of nations.[9]

The Powers Under Christ

Paul's belief in delegated spiritual powers, then, was rather routine in the first-century Hellenistic world. But the *way* in which he viewed them was unique. For he related them, as he did everything else, to the blinding revelation of the Messiah which he received on the road to Da-

---

[8]Also found in Gal 4:3 and Col 2:8, 20, where the NRSV translates it "elemental spirits of the world [universe]."

[9]*De mutatione nominum* 8. For an excellent survey of Hellenistic religious background, see Daniel G. Reid, "Elements/Elemental Spirits of the World" and "Principalities and Powers," in *Dictionary of Paul and His Letters: A Compendium of Contemporary Biblical Scholarship,* ed. Gerald F. Hawthorne, Ralph P. Martin and Daniel G. Reid (Downers Grove, Ill.: InterVarsity Press, 1993), pp. 229-32, 746-52.

mascus. There, and after, he came to see the Messiah as the principal agent of creation, who at his crucifixion defeated the fallen powers and now ruled them from his throne at the top of the cosmos, as it were.

This new conviction of Christ's lordship over all the powers is the only way to make good sense of a number of tricky passages in Paul's letters. It helps explain what Paul meant by "those not being by nature gods" (Gal 4:8) whom the Galatians nevertheless had "served" before they became Christians (Gal 4:3, 8), and "so-called gods" in his letter to Corinth (1 Cor 8:5). Paul calls these same beings the "weak and beggarly *stoicheia*" (Gal 4:9; cf. the same word in Col 2:8, 20).

In other words, Paul was telling his churches that the star deities which the Greeks worshiped were in reality the same national angels whom Daniel identified as malevolent powers now hostile to God's people but to be defeated in the last days.[10] They were created by the preexistent Christ (Col 1:16), led in triumphal procession as defeated enemies at the cross (Col 2:15), subjected invisibly but decisively at that point to the triumphant and ruling Christ (Eph 1:21; Col 2:10), will one day acknowledge to the cosmos that they are indeed subservient to Christ (Phil 2:10), and will be defeated finally at the end of this world (1 Cor 15:24).

Werner Foerster explains that these angelic beings are cosmic powers, not demons. Paul refers to these angelic powers as *archontes* and *exousiai* (principalities and powers), not *daimones* or *daimonia*, which are the words used commonly by the New Testament for demons or local spirits that afflict individuals. *Daimones* and *daimonia* are restricted to the "air," the lowest region of the earth and sky which humans inhabit, while *exousiai* and *archontes* are given authority over entire nations. Foerster adds that *thronoi* and *kyriotētes* (two other words Paul uses for spiritual powers, usually translated as "thrones" and "dominions") may stand immediately in the presence of God, in the highest heavens. (We know that Paul believed in ascending levels of heavens because of his autobiographical description of a "person in Christ . . . caught up to the *third* heaven" [2 Cor 12:2, emphasis mine].)[11]

---

[10]This may be how a first-century Jew like Paul would have interpreted Judges 5:20: "The stars fought from heaven."

[11]Werner Foerster, "ἐξουσία," in *Theological Dictionary of the New Testament [TDNT]*, ed. Gerhard Kittel (Grand Rapids: Eerdmans, 1964), 2:573.

It seems clear, then, that Paul believed in spiritual powers that had a limited potency in the world, and that these were not the demons so frequently mentioned in the gospels. We see more of Paul's understanding of these powers in an intriguing passage in 1 Corinthians 2. Here Paul uses a form of the word *archontes* (at this point, "rulers").

> Yet among the mature we do speak wisdom, though it is not a wisdom of this age or of the *rulers* of this age, who are doomed to perish. But we speak God's wisdom, secret and hidden, which God decreed before the ages for our glory. None of the *rulers* of this age understood this; for if they had, they would not have crucified the Lord of glory. (1 Cor 2:6-8)

Some interpreters have insisted that Paul's "rulers" here are merely the human authorities who killed Jesus. But then why would Paul say they "are doomed to perish"? No one ever doubted the mortality of human rulers. But they did doubt the mortality of the *spiritual* rulers and principalities. Besides, the same Greek word is used in the fifteenth chapter of this same letter, where the "rulers" are clearly spiritual. They are "enemies," and one of them is "death" itself (1 Cor 15:24-26). It appears, then, that these rulers were spiritual powers whom Paul believed were responsible for killing Jesus of Nazareth.

The more interesting question this passage raises, however, is not the existence of spiritual powers but why they would have been so stupid! Notice that Paul says that "none of the rulers of this age" understood God's plan and therefore proceeded to crucify the "Lord of glory." If they were cosmic spiritual powers, wouldn't they have realized that Jesus was the Son of God and that killing him would mean trouble for them?

Not if they had misunderstood their roles, and therefore God's plan. The powers apparently believed that with God's separation from humanity after the Fall because of human sin (Rom 1:24-28), they would become unconditional world rulers *(kosmokratores)*. Sin had established a "wall of partition" between God and humans, leaving the powers free from God's interference to govern human beings according to the harsh regime of divine law.[12]

George Caird has explained that, for Paul, the powers ruled by their

---

[12]Gerhard Delling, "ἀρχή," in *TDNT,* 1:483.

manipulation of God's legal system.[13] They used (1) human obligation to obey the law and (2) God's just demand to punish the law's violations to hold human beings in bondage. That is why Paul said that "the power of sin is the law" and "sin, seizing an opportunity in the commandment, produced in me all kinds of covetousness" (1 Cor 15:56; Rom 7:8). The powers used God's holy law to keep humans "enslaved" not only to sin but also to the powers' false religion (Gal 4:8, 10), which in turn diverted human beings from true religion. As long as the powers could convince human beings that law is God's final word, they could continue to masquerade as absolute gods rather than merely angelic delegates. And the powers themselves could continue to believe that their dominion over humanity would last forever. Human beings continued to believe there was no way out of a system of law that brought only condemnation for their sins.

But at Christ's crucifixion and resurrection, the powers' deception was unmasked—to their horror and Paul's delight. Now it became clear that God's punitive legal system was going to be superceded by grace; that when law is isolated and exalted into an independent system of religion, it becomes demonic. But a new regime of grace would be inaugurated precisely by an enactment of the legal regime: death was administered as punishment for sin (which the powers rightly believed was necessary), but through the death of the Son of God. His resurrection vindicated the plan, showing "to the rulers and authorities in the heavenly places" God's wisdom and "eternal purpose" (Eph 3:10-11). That is, now the powers saw that "the record that stood against us with its legal demands" was erased; Christ "set this aside, nailing it to the cross" by fulfilling in his own body what it required (Col 2:14). The powers now realized that they would lose their hold over those human subjects who identified with a new organic unity (the body of the risen Christ) over which evil has no power.

Hence by his crucifixion and resurrection Christ "disarmed the rulers and authorities, and made a public example of them, triumphing over them in it" (Col 2:15). The powers now saw their cosmic error in conspiring to execute Jesus. They had imagined they would eliminate the

---

[13]Caird, *Principalities and Powers*.

greatest threat to their rule by killing the divine interloper. Instead they opened the door to their destroyer. By fulfilling God's law, Christ showed the powers that law was not God's last word. This disarmed the powers, because they kept their human subjects in bondage by the deception that law and its condemnation was the entirety of religion. They also kept their subjects captive by the power of sin, which used law to make its hold even more tenacious. But Christ's complete obedience, performed vicariously for human subjects, broke the powers' hold. Because Christ was not only divine but also a man, sharing human nature, his *human* obedience could set aside "the record that stood against us with its legal demands" (Col 2:14). For now the legal demands had been fulfilled. His human obedience became our human obedience because he shared our humanity.

Now, therefore, all the cosmos was beginning to see that grace, not law, is God's ultimate word. All the angelic and human creatures were coming to learn that law was only meant to lead them to Christ's rule of grace (Gal 3:24). God had permitted people to die through the law—even through the delegation of legal power to corrupted beings!—so that he could make them alive by grace through justification (God's acceptance of humans because of what Christ did). He did that by accepting one man's obedience as counting for the obedience of all—thereby setting all free from having to serve the system that regarded law as the only word.

And last but not least, this new understanding of God's ways with humanity also exposed the powers as the corrupted "weak and beggarly spirits" that they were, not the absolute gods they claimed to be (Gal 4:9). The powers were thus shown to be "usurpers of the divine majesty and imposters in the claims they made upon man's allegiance."[14]

Defeated but Alive and Active

But if the powers were exposed and defeated by that exposé, they were not stripped of all power. They continued to inspire both persecutors of God's people (Paul no doubt thought of the prince of Persia who secretly instigated Persian attacks on Jews in Daniel 10) and moral temp-

---

[14]Ibid., p. 85.

tation regularly afflicting Christian believers. In fact, the powers' chief leader, "the ruler of the power of the air," was "now at work among those who are disobedient" (Eph 2:2).

Does this sound implausible? That defeated powers could still hold on to power? Recall from the last chapter our comparison to D-day. This analogy was originally suggested by the New Testament scholar Oscar Cullman.[15] After the June 1944 invasion at Normandy, France, the Axis powers knew they were, for all practical purposes, defeated. They knew the question was not *if* but *when* they would finally be compelled to lay down their arms. But on they fought, with whatever weapons they still possessed, for almost another year, killing hundreds of thousands of allied soldiers. Interestingly, more British and American soldiers died *after* D-day than before. Which is analogous to the cross. Although the cross defeated Satan and the powers, they have done more harm to more people in history *since* that time than before. But they were defeated nonetheless, and the final manifestation of that defeat will come one day in the future.

Similarly, the powers were shown their final end at the cross, but they still hold on to some of their weapons and power. They are alive and well among enemies of the church, orchestrating their nefarious attacks on true religion and forces of righteousness. Paul probably imagined that, just as they inspired the Roman and Jewish authorities who killed Jesus, they were now lurking behind Roman and Jewish officials who continued to hound Christian believers. Christians' real enemies, then, were not people. "We wrestle not against flesh and blood . . ." Their real foes were spiritual, the same kind of invisible forces that bedeviled Jews for centuries—fallen angelic beings who masquerade as gods but are actually malign forces conspiring against God's people and his kingdom.[16] "Our struggle is not against enemies of blood and flesh, but against the rulers, against the authorities, against the cosmic powers of this present darkness, against the spiritual forces of evil in the heavenly places" (Eph 6:12).

But if the powers continue to do their dirty work, they won't be able

---

[15]Oscar Cullman, *Christ and Time* (London: SCM Press, 1962).
[16]This is the New Testament's interpretation of the OT's sometimes bewildering variety of ways to interpret "the gods."

to do it forever. When Jesus returns again to earth and the present world comes to an end, judgment will come for all, including the powers. Along with wicked men and women, they too will be judged and condemned. Like all the rest of God's enemies, they will be put "under his feet" (1 Cor 15:25). Even their knees will bow, and their tongues will confess "that Jesus Christ is Lord, to the glory of God the Father" (Phil 2:10-11).

In the meantime, Christians will be protected against the powers' worst designs, which are to separate them from Christ. Paul promises that even in the worst "distress, or persecution, or famine, . . . or peril" (Rom 8:35) none of the evil powers will be able to separate true believers from the love of their Lord Christ:

> For I am convinced that neither death, nor life, nor *angels,* nor *rulers [ar-chai],* nor things present, nor things to come, nor *powers [dynameis],* nor height, nor depth, nor anything else in all creation, will be able to separate us from the love of God in Christ Jesus our Lord. (Rom 8:38-39, emphasis added)

The Dialectical Roles of the Law, the State and Satan

In the Pauline correspondence, then, we have what scholars call a dialectical view of the powers. This means that to understand them properly, we have to go back and forth between two apparently contradictory poles. They are both good and bad. They were created good, but have gone bad. They are used by God for his good purposes, such as enforcing respect for his law. But they also distort the meaning of that law and lead people away from the true God by masquerading as the supreme deity.

Paul clearly sees them as diabolical and nefarious, but at the same time he hints they may be redeemable. Ephesians 3:10 says that part of God's plan is to make known his wisdom "to the rulers and authorities in the heavenly places," and the first chapter of that epistle asserts that God's "plan" won't be completed until all things in "the *heavens*" and the earth are brought together in Christ (Eph 1:10). In his prison letter to the Philippians, Paul predicts that every knee in "the *heavens*" will bow, and every tongue confess, that the Lord is Jesus Christ (Eph 2:10-11).

Don't get me wrong. These proclamations do not clearly claim that the powers will eventually be reconciled. They are no more than hints. The church has never known with assurance their future, and scholars are divided on this question.

But we might be able to understand this issue a bit better, and the dialectical role of the powers more generally, by looking at other intermediaries in God's administration—law itself, the state and even Satan.

As we have seen, God's law also plays a dialectical role in God's way of working with human beings. It is positive and good when it takes a secondary position in the service of grace, which was God's first word to the creation. Paul explains that the promise of grace was first and original, and that the law came only later, because of sin. Law becomes twisted and demonic only when it is treated as primary and absolute (Gal 3:15-24).

In its secondary roles, however, law serves God's purposes. It serves as God's attorney, accusing sinners of their sins (Rom 2:12; 3:19); it carries out God's sentence of death (2 Cor 3:6-7). Sin (a power in itself) uses law to tyrannize, and God in turn uses that tyranny as a punishment for those who reject him (Rom 1:24). So the tyranny of sin, using law as its jailer, is both the work of sin against God and the work of God to eventually destroy sin. Law, then, is God's "strange work," which his wrath uses to kill, in order that he can also give life. Law is an intermediary, created good by God, used for evil purposes for a time, but in the long run used by God to serve his ultimate purposes (Rom 10:4). Like the spiritual powers.

Let's look also at the state. Like the powers, it gets its authority from God (Rom 13:1-7) and is a "servant of God" (Rom 13:4). In 2 Thessalonians 2:7 it is probably the "restraining power" that holds back the "mystery of lawlessness." Paul knew that it was the state that prevented Caligula from erecting a statue of himself in the temple in 40 C.E., and that protected Paul himself from Jews seeking to kill him (Acts 23). But when the state regarded its derived authority as primary and absolute, it became demonic. Paul and every other Christian of the first century remembered that it was the best of all states (Rome) that had crucified the Christ.

Even Satan follows this pattern of delegated powers. Paul was a student of the Old Testament, and the Old Testament Satan was God's public prosecutor. In Job 1—2 his job is to resist evildoers. He is one of the sons of Elohim (Hebrew for "God") and has access to the heavenly court. In 1 Chronicles 21:1 Satan incites David to take a census, but apparently in the name of God—for in 2 Samuel 24:1 it is "God" who is said to have incited David. Do you see the picture? Satan is a creation of God enforcing God's law through a "ministry" of accusation. His job is to defend justice according to God's law. But, as we have seen before, he treats law, which is secondary in God's final order, as primary.

Satan's role is like that of other law-enforcers, such as the angel of death or the angels of punishment. The psalmist writes of the "destroying angels" in Psalm 78:49 who poured out God's wrath on the Egyptians. Like the state, they are instruments of God's wrath and justice (Rom 13:4). Of course, Satan is unique. He may make accurate accusations against human beings, but about God and his ways he is a deceiver (2 Cor 11:3, 14). Nevertheless, he is another example of created intermediaries who, while attempting their own mischief, are exploited by God for his higher purposes. As Paul's Jewish contemporary Philo put it, God rules through intermediate powers, who are servants to do things not appropriate to God himself.[17]

What About the Gospels?

Perhaps at this point you're wondering why I have not mentioned the gospels. The answer is that while this idea of God working through intermediate powers is not absent from the gospels, it is most fully developed by Paul.

But the same structure is present in the gospels. Jesus says there are "powers" *(dynameis)* in the heavens that will see the Son of Man when he comes on the clouds (Mk 13:25-26); they will be shaken on that day (Mt 24:29). The power of the powers has already been broken; while they continue to harass and obstruct, they will be finally abolished at the end of time (Mt 13:24-30). Jesus offers proof that their power has been broken by his exorcisms, which demonstrate his binding of the powers' evil chief, Satan (Mk 3:27; par. Lk 11:22; cf. Lk 10:19). In John's gospel, Satan's defeat is linked to the cross (Jn 14:30; 16:11).

So although the picture is not as fleshed out, the Gospels outline es-

---

[17] *Confessions* 36.

sentially the same picture that Paul drew in more detail: the cosmos is full of intermediate powers that were created good by God, but which at some point turned against God and are now actively hostile. Yet their power was broken at the cross, and God is now using them, even as they fight ferociously against his kingdom, to advance his own larger agenda. They will finally be defeated fully at the end of time.

In Sum: Paul on the Religions

So what does all this have to do with the religions? What do the powers say to us about Paul's approaches to other religions?

A good way to sum up is to look at Paul's personal encounter with other religions in Athens. It was about the year 50 when Paul sailed down from northern Greece to reach Athens. His ship probably docked at the port of Piraeus, from which he walked five miles on the Hamaxitos Road through the Dipylon Gate and on to the Acropolis. All along the way, on street corners and in niches and temples, he saw beautiful works of art depicting gods and demigods.

But Paul, rather than appreciating their beauty, was "provoked" (Acts 17:16 NASB). The Greek word Luke uses is the one from which we get *paroxysm*. Paul, like all conscientious Jews, was deeply disturbed by pagan idolatry. So he went to the synagogue, where he probably found sympathy for the horror he felt. If he found Jews with whom to commiserate, however, it didn't stop him from spending several days arguing with his Jewish brothers about Jesus. Luke tells us he did the same in the marketplace.

There he met Epicurean and Stoic philosophers, who referred to him as a "babbler" and said, probably with sarcasm, that he was preaching "foreign divinities" (Acts 17:18). Luke goes out of his way to return the favor by saying sardonically that these Greek philosophers "would spend their time in nothing but telling or hearing something new" (Acts 17:21).

Then Paul stood up in the middle of the Areopagus, the venerable meeting place on top of a rocky hill near the Acropolis and marketplace, and preached a sermon. For our purposes, it is worth noting that the sermon was full of derogatory references to Greek religion, centering on the notion of human ignorance. He chose to talk about an altar he had noticed "to an unknown god," and corrected a host of religious notions which no doubt were held by some Athenians: that God lives in temples, could be served by human hands, is distant, is like gold or silver or stone, and can be represented by an artistic image (Acts 17:23-29).

Some interpreters have tried to rescue Paul's speech for interreligious dialogue by pointing to Paul's statement about pagans getting to God:

> From one ancestor [God] made all nations to inhabit the whole earth, and he allotted the times of their existence and the boundaries of the places where they would live, so that they would search for God and *perhaps grope for him and find him.* (Acts 17:26-27, emphasis added)

These interpreters have keyed on that last phrase, claiming that Paul suggested by these words that pagans can find God through their own religions. The problem, however, is twofold: first, the context of the whole sermon is decidedly pessimistic about the ability of any Greek religion to provide knowledge of God. Second, the Greek word for "grope" (ψηλαφήσειαν) "denotes the groping and fumbling of a blind man."[18] Besides, the grammatical construction of those last six words is an optative clause (expressing wishing or hoping), which when combined with the Greek word for "grope," probably means Paul thought it unlikely that any seekers actually found God in these religions.

Paul concludes by saying that while in the past God had overlooked times of *ignorance,* now he commands all people everywhere to repent. Judgment is at hand. And the proof of that was Jesus' resurrection (Acts 17:30-31). In other words, Paul came face to face with the religion of cultured civilization, and he concluded that it is a miasma of ignorance that leads to idolatry.

This shouldn't be surprising, because we have already seen that Paul saw bent powers lurking behind the world's political and religious institutions. It is clear, then, that Paul believed the origins of non-Jewish and non-Christian religion lay in pride and deception. Angelic powers that had been created to serve God instead chose in their pride to rebel. Then they enticed whole populations to worship them instead of God,

---

[18]Charles S. C. Williams, *A Commentary on the Acts of the Apostles* (New York: Harper & Row, 1958), p. 204.

and distorted what they knew of God's truth in the process. Using God's holy law, they held their devotees as prisoners (Gal 3:23). Therefore, when Christians participated in pagan worship at their temples, they were actually consorting with powers of darkness, or what Paul called "demons." Paul, therefore, took a hard line against other religions. He seems to have believed they were creations of deception and malice, from whose worship and rituals Christians must steer clear.

But is that the sum total of Paul's attitude toward other religions? Not really. Paul's sermon at the Areopagus contains hints of a certain recognition of truth in the religions that dovetails with what we have already seen. Two points can be noted. First, Paul suggests in this sermon that these Athenian pagans, while mired in religious ignorance, were nevertheless groping for the same God whom Paul knew to be the Father of Jesus Christ. He tells them, "What therefore you worship as unknown, this I proclaim to you" (Acts 17:23). In other words, while their ideas about God were nearly all wrong, nevertheless the object of their misguided worship was still the same God who had revealed himself to Paul as the true and living God.

Second, Paul acknowledges that some Greek poets, presumably devotees of false Greek religion, spoke religious truth.

> For "in him we live and move and have our being"; as even some of your own poets have said,
>   "For we too are his offspring." (Acts 17:28)

Paul was probably quoting Epimenides (6th century B.C.E.) and Aratus (4th century B.C.E.). The astonishing thing to note here is that Paul, who apparently believed that Greek religion was abysmally ignorant of the true God, nevertheless conceded—in a sermon highlighting Greek religious ignorance!—that the religions had *some* access to *some* true notions of the living God.

These two gleanings from this remarkable sermon on Mars Hill (a translation of "Areopagus"), when connected to what Paul believed about the powers, suggest a few promising threads which a student of Paul can use to stitch together the beginnings of a theology that would answer the question of this book: Why are there other religions?

Remember what we have already learned: The power behind the religions, for Paul, consists in angelic powers that were originally created good but fell from grace. They use God's law in a cynical way to enforce fidelity to their own worship, and in the process distort the meaning of divine law. Like other intermediary powers that are fallen, they have taken what is good and holy and used it for unholy ends.

Yet in the process, some truth emerges. Human beings under their thrall still learn something of God's truth and law. They still learn that they are not autonomous but created subjects who are accountable and will face judgment. Like the powers behind national states, the powers behind the religions perhaps restrain other forms of evil that would otherwise reduce civilization to violent anarchy. Some of them teach the truths that God is supreme over the cosmos and stands for justice and goodness—though of course they define those terms in ways that sometimes conflict with Christian notions.

In sum, then, a Pauline approach can say that while the religions originated in rebellion and deception, their origins are supernatural, not natural; they teach some truth about God; and they are used by God to advance his own plan of redemption. This approach could even go so far as to say that God might be using precisely their miscues to teach otherwise unteachable lessons to his people. For if Paul said that the powers used the law to keep people in bondage, and yet at the same time the law led them to Christ, perhaps the religions also, in all of their error and deception, are leading God's people to truth about Christ that otherwise is unattainable.

This is the sort of approach that the Greek theologians took in the next two centuries after Paul. They believed that other religions, particularly Platonic approaches to God which we lump under the term "philosophy," contained divinely ordained approaches that not only led the ancients part way to God, but also possessed clues for Christians who want to understand God better.

5

SEEDS OF THE WORD

Justin Martyr on Seeds of the Word in Other Religions

IT WAS A BEAUTIFUL SPRING MORNING IN EPHESUS, in the year 131
C.E. Justin had come out to a lonely field overlooking the Aegean Sea,
where he often came to clear his head and try to think great thoughts.
His Platonist teacher had told him that if he could lift his mind above the
world of sense and focus on immaterial forms, he would eventually be
able to "look upon God."[1]

Justin was a seeker, twenty-six years old. He had grown up in
Shechem (now Nablus in the West Bank), an ancient settlement in Palestine, the land of the Jews. He wasn't a Jew himself, and he knew little
about their religion. But their passion for God inspired him to try to find
God for himself, using the Greco-Roman philosophies of his day.

In the second century "philosophy" was its own kind of religion, devoted to seeking God. That's why his teacher, a disciple of Plato, had
promised him a vision of God if he would only be diligent. Justin had
already tried other teachers and found them wanting. The Stoic master
neither knew God nor had any interest in the search. The Peripatetic
(teacher of Aristotle's thought) seemed more interested in fame and fees
than knowledge of God. The Pythagorean insisted that Justin first learn
music, astronomy and geometry. But Justin was impatient. So when he
found a Platonist tutor who suggested he could get right to divine contemplation, Justin was ecstatic.

But on this spectacular morning walk, as his eyes feasted on the azure

---

[1]The following story is my own loose retelling of Justin's account of his conversion in his *Dialogue with Trypho,* chaps. 2-6.

ocean set against a deep blue sky, he was startled by a strange sight. An old man had been following him, in this field where he had never seen another soul. The man looked respectable enough. His garments were neither extravagant nor raggedy. The lines and expression on his face suggested thoughtfulness, but without any hint of arrogance.

"Why are you staring at me, young man?"

"I'm sorry sir, I didn't mean to. I was just surprised to see anyone here. I thought I was the only one who knew about this place."

The man smiled. "Well, I don't usually come over here. But I'm looking for one of my nephews who has wandered off. What brings *you* here so often?"

"I like to come here because it is so quiet and I can be all alone." Proudly, he volunteered, "I use this field to concentrate on philology." [Philology means "love for words."]

The old man frowned. "So you love words more than goodness or truth? You're a sophist, then?"

"Not at all! I do love words, but especially the words that go to the heart of things. Surely you wouldn't disagree that it is the Logos [literally, "Word"] that gives form to everything that exists?"

"I wouldn't disagree."

"So then you would also agree that if Word is the key to everything, understanding *words* will help us see what is the Cause of everything? And that then we can see what is really true, and be able to pick out the errors in so much thinking today?"

"Perhaps, perhaps. But don't be so sure that you can get so easily from a study of words to true knowledge of the Word that is the Cause of all that exists." The old man began to ask Justin questions about God and the Word, continuing in Socratic manner, to explain that there are some things even a wise philosopher cannot know by reason unless he hears from someone who has seen those things. "Like an animal in India that is different from any animal ever seen around these lands—an animal you'd never imagine unless you had seen it."

Justin was puzzled. "But God cannot be seen. He can be discerned only by the mind, as Plato said, and I believe him."

The old man nodded. "Do you really think man's little mind can see the infinite God—without illumination by God's own spirit?"

"Well, Plato said it can. He said there is an affinity in the mind for God, as long as the mind really desires it."

"But is the mind ever pure enough to desire it rightly?"

"If it has been trained by moral virtue."

"Let's see, then," the old man replied impishly. "Since goats and sheep are pure in their intentions, without any trace of animosity toward others, they can see God."

"Don't be silly. Of course they can't. They don't have enough reason to overcome the impediment of their bodies."

The old man then used a long chain of Socratic question-and-answer to prove that bodies are not reincarnated, as Plato said they were. Neither are souls preexistent, he explained. For uncreated souls must be like God, and so would not sin. But we all know that every human being sins repeatedly.

After explaining that souls must get their life from a Being who is the source of all life, Justin realized that this old man might know more about God than even Plato. "Please, dear sir, tell me how I can learn about God, if, as you suggest, even the greatest Platonists cannot tell me what I want to know."

The old man told Justin about the Jewish prophets who, long before Plato and Pythagoras, were told by God's own Spirit things that reason could never apprehend on its own. And that they accurately predicted the coming of the Messiah—the Christ, the Son of God—who was the embodiment of the Logos, Reason in human flesh.

The old man left after these words, and Justin never saw him again. But "straightaway a flame was kindled in my soul; and a love of the prophets, and of those men who are friends of Christ, possessed me."

Justin went on to become a Christian and then a distinguished Christian teacher, first at Ephesus and then in Rome. In the empire's capital, above the public baths, he held classes for inquirers, wearing the cloak of a philosopher (the *pallium*). From Rome he wrote many important works, but only three have survived: two *Apologies,* the first addressed to the emperor Antoninus Pius and his adopted sons (Marcus Aurelius was one), and his *Dialogue with Trypho* (supposedly a Jewish interlocutor). He and six of his disciples were denounced as Christians about the year 165, probably by a jealous Cynic philosopher whom Justin had bested in public debate. On refusing to sacrifice to the gods, they were tortured and beheaded. Ever since, the Christian philosopher from Palestine has been known as Justin Martyr.

Philosophy as Religion

Justin became a Christian when he concluded that Plato could not lead him to God. But he is important for our study, ironically, because of what he later concluded Plato *did* know of God.

Remember, the ancient world's conception of philosophy was very different from our own. We typically think, with some good reason, that philosophy is for those who have given up on religion. So if you want to find God, you would not go first to the philosophers. But in the second century, most religious seekers pursued Greek philosophy with the intent of finding God, or whatever it was that answered the big questions about life. As Justin put it, "The duty of philosophy is to investigate the Deity."[2]

There was good reason then to turn to Pythagoras and Plato and Aristotle. They asked the big questions, including whether there was a god, what we can know about that god, and how to live accordingly. They also wrote about politics and science and logic, but these disciplines were related to life in a cosmos whose meaning could not be found apart from the God question. In the ancient world, then, there was no sharp division—as there is today—between philosophy and religion. Of course there were Greeks and Romans who looked more to the myths of assorted gods and goddesses for meaning and morals. But even some of them believed that Socrates and Plato and Aristotle found a unity behind the conflicting particularities of the myths—and that the unity was as much religious as it was philosophical.[3]

So when Justin wrote about the philosophers, he was really talking about other religions—other ways of construing God and the gods. Justin had a lot to say about these other religions. And as he thought of

---

[2] *Dialogue with Trypho* 1. This and other translations of the two *Apologies* are taken from *The Writings of Justin Martyr and Athenagoras,* ed. Marcus Dods et al. (Edinburgh: T & T Clark, 1879).

[3] At the same time that Justin and many other early Christian writers saw broken truth in Greek philosophy, most condemned the details and general direction of Greek and Roman *religions,* particularly their polytheism and immorality.

these different, and in some cases rival, ways of thinking about God, he came up with some fresh ideas—so innovative that he has been called "one of the most original thinkers Christianity produced."[4]

Old Themes: Gods as Angels Who Transgressed

But first, let's look at the ways in which Justin picked up themes from the Old Testament and Paul which we have already seen. They will show us how powerful these ideas were in the ancient Jewish and Christian worlds, and that they continued to resonate with the early church even a century after its beginning. In other words, early Christians were deeply influenced by the ways the biblical writers portrayed other religions.

The first biblical themes we see in Justin are the ideas that (1) God set various angels over the nations and (2) the angels overstepped the bounds set for them.

"At the creation," Justin wrote in his *Second Apology,* God "committed the care of men and of all things under heaven to *angels* whom He appointed over them." But the angels "transgressed their appointment," led astray by sexual desire. Inspired no doubt by Genesis 6:2 and Jude 6,[5] Justin says these wayward angels "were captivated by the love of women, and begat children who are those that are called demons."[6]

Justin added a riff on yet another biblical motif—that these rebellious angels masqueraded as gods who bound to themselves whole populations with new religious rites and rules empowered by fear.

> They afterwards subdued the human race to themselves, partly by magical writings, and partly by fears and punishments they occasioned, and partly by teaching them to offer sacrifices, and incense, and libations.[7]

The result of all this pagan religion, set on divine foundations but then corrupted by angelic interlopers, was moral chaos. Justin attributed the history of human evil to this strange religious brew: "Among men [the

---

[4] E. F. Osborn, *Justin Martyr* (Tübingen: Mohr, 1973), p. 201.

[5] "The sons of God [lit., "sons of Elohim"] saw that the daughters of man were attractive. And they took as their wives any they chose" (Gen 6:2 ESV). "The angels who did not keep their own position, but left their proper dwelling . . . indulged in sexual immorality and pursued unnatural lust" (Jude 6-7).

[6] *Second Apology* 5.

[7] *Second Apology* 5.

seditious angels] sowed murders, wars, adulteries, intemperate deeds, and all wickedness."[8]

Old Themes: Demons in the Shadows

Justin also learned from Paul that behind the pagan religious rites lay sinister demons. We just saw that Justin believed demons were the offspring of mutinous angels. Apparently he also believed that while the national angels established themselves as the gods of pagan religions, they assigned the maintenance of their religions to their demonic offspring. And the demons' most powerful tool, which fixed men and women to these religions, was fear. They show "fearful sights" to their human subjects, especially those who do not use reason properly, and use sexual perversion to corrupt their devotees.

> For the truth shall be spoken; since of old these evil demons, effecting apparitions of themselves, both defiled women and corrupted boys, and showed such fearful sights to men, that those who did not use their reason in judging of the actions that were done, were struck with terror; and being carried away by fear, and not knowing that these were demons, they called them gods.[9]

A New Theme: The Prisca Theologia

So far, Justin's treatment of other gods and religions has been fairly commonplace. For the most part he reiterates things we saw in Deuteronomy, the Psalms, Daniel and Paul. God originally intended diverse angels to care for the nations beyond Israel, but some of these angels decided to go their own way. Heavenly creatures then persuaded human creatures that the former were creators, with the result that the latter became fearful slaves instead of happy subjects. Non-Jewish and now non-Christian religion is therefore a tale of deception and bondage.

But Justin made some significant departures. He added some new themes that cast the religions in an entirely new light. If Paul saw the religions in largely negative terms—the dark arena of demons from which are emitted occasional glimmers of light—Justin was far more

---

[8] Second Apology 5.
[9] First Apology 5.

positive: popular religion, demonic though it is, yet contains some truth, and philosophical religion is in fact often inspired by none other than Christ himself.

But I am getting ahead of myself. I need to explain Justin's innovations one at a time. First was his development of the *prisca theologia* (lit., the "ancient theology"). Justin was probably the first Christian thinker to appropriate a tradition, started by both Greeks and Jews, that claimed massive borrowing from one tradition to another. Long before Justin, Pythagoreans had represented Plato as the great popularizer of his predecessor Pythagoras. They claimed Plato had visited Pythagorean schools in southern Italy.

Jews made a similar move, asserting that the Greeks themselves had learned from Moses. The great Philo, Paul's contemporary, confidently maintained that Greek philosophers depended on the Pentateuch. At the beginning of the second century, the Jewish historian Josephus wrote *Against Apion,* both to rebut critics of his *Antiquities* and to combat anti-Semitic prejudices. Part of his defense of Jewish culture was an elaborate attempt to prove the antiquity of Jewish religion and Greek dependence on it. As evidence, he and other Jewish apologists cited the story by Plato's biographer that the Greek philosopher visited Egypt, where, according to Jewish interpreters, he had read the Pentateuch, or at least been instructed by learned rabbis.[10] Even some later Greeks accepted this story. Numenius of Apamea, a Neopythagorean contemporary of Justin, affirmed Greek dependence on Jewish sources when he asked, "What is Plato but Moses in Attic Greek?"[11]

Later Christians decried this borrowing as unethical plagiarism. But for Justin, Plato's use of Moses was to be commended. Even the demons should be credited for their partial understanding. They too copied from the Jewish Bible. They misunderstood much of it, but the parts they got right show up in pagan myths as dim reflections of biblical stories. They read, for example, in Genesis 49:11 about the prince of Judah, who "washes . . . his robe in the blood of grapes," and blended it with the Christian story of the Son of God's passion and ascension. Since the chief of de-

---

[10]Henry Chadwick, *Early Christian Thought and the Classical Tradition: Studies in Justin, Clement, and Origen* (New York: Oxford University Press, 1966), pp. 13-14.

[11]Quoted by Clement of Alexandria, *Stromata* 1.150.4; Chadwick, *Early Christian Thought,* p. 15.

mons, the devil, had already given the name Bacchus to one of his divine masquerades, these reports from his demons helped flesh out the character of the new deity. The result was the myth that "Bacchus was the son of Jupiter . . . the discoverer of the vine . . . [with] wine among his mysteries . . . [and] that, having been torn in pieces, he ascended into heaven."[12]

The devil, with the assistance of his junior demons, did the same thing for Hercules and Aesculapius. Using the prophecies of Isaiah and Daniel, these demonic plagiarizers concocted the mysteries of Mithras. They also imitated the Christian Eucharist, prescribing bread and water with certain incantations for Mithraic initiation ceremonies.[13]

But if demons unwittingly scatter breadcrumbs of truth among their poisons, they maliciously plot to divert humans away from the truth. According to Justin, they heard from the Jewish prophets that the Son of God would come as Messiah and that the ungodly would be punished by fire. So they "put forward many to be called sons of Jupiter" teaching analogous things, so that the Christian stories then appeared to be "mere marvelous tales, like the things which were said by the poets."[14] In other words, demons minted counterfeit religion in order to cheapen true religion. Like skilled printers of bogus money, they hoped to flood the market with so many ersatz bills that seekers would confuse the imitation for the divine original.

Not only do the demons use echoes of biblical truth to deceive their human devotees, but they also inspire these devotees to persecute Christians. They get pagans to harass Christians by convincing them that Christian warnings of future punishment are laughable and by raising up heretics like Marcion who denounce Christian doctrine.[15] Justin was writing in an era when Christians were often tortured and killed. The best explanation for otherwise decent people turning against harmless citizens seemed to be the invisible maneuverings of malign spiritual forces. In fact, it also explained Jesus' crucifixion: demons incited Jews to kill their own Messiah.[16]

---

[12]*First Apology* 54.
[13]*Dialogue with Trypho* 49, 70.
[14]*First Apology* 54.
[15]*First Apology* 57, 58.
[16]*First Apology* 63.

But if demons practice a pale reflection of the *prisca theologia,* the Greek philosophers did a far better job. And their motives were not so nefarious. Without the intent to mislead and redirect from the truth, philosophers led seekers closer to the true God by what they learned from the Hebrew Scriptures. Plato, for instance, learned from Moses that the world is not eternal but was created at some point in time. And from messianic hints in those sacred writings Plato determined that there is a power next to God that is placed crosswise in the universe. From other clues he figured there must be a third entity in the divine. He did not understand these things with a great deal of accuracy, but it was his sitting at the feet of Moses that explained these remarkable pointers to Christian truth.[17]

A New Theme: Seeds of the Word Among All Reasonable Persons

Learning from the Jews was only one explanation for remarkable religious truth among the philosophers, and even among some popular religious myths and rites. Justin advanced a second explanation far more novel and promising: pagans were learning from Christ himself in his role as the Logos or Word of the cosmos. Here Justin developed an idea first suggested by the apostle John, that Jesus was the Logos, who not only created the world and holds it together moment-by-moment but also "enlightens everyone." John traded on the Stoic concept of a logos or rational principle that gave form to all the creation and is discernible because it is present in the human mind (Jn 1:1, 9).

Justin pushed this Johannine concept further by relating it to the religions. He argued, in effect, that Christ the Logos was speaking in the philosophical religions of the Hellenistic world. Socrates, he said, knew Christ in part because he had part of the Logos. Christ "was and is the Logos who is in every man," and so inspires whatever truth we find in the world.[18] Therefore "whatever things were rightly said among all men, are the property of us Christians."[19]

Drawing on Jesus' parable of the sower, Justin contended that the Sto-

---

[17] *First Apology* 59, 54.
[18] *Second Apology* 10.
[19] Ibid., 10, 13.

ics, the poets and the historians all "spoke well in proportion to the share [they] had of the seminal divine Logos *[tou spermatikou theiou logou]*." They were all "able to see realities darkly through the sowing of the implanted words that was in them."[20] They could see, for example, Christian truths such as the creation, final judgment and even the Trinity.

So the word of Christ, speaking to non-Christians, explains whatever truth there is in other religions. It also explains why there is error in the religions. "Because they did not know the whole Logos, which is Christ, they often contradicted themselves."[21] With only part of the Logos, they could not see the whole picture. They could see the trees but not the forest; details without the big picture; truths taken out of context; little nuggets of gold, but without the means to cash them in.

Justin went still further, making claims that were daring for the second century. Not only did he say that some non-Christian thinkers had parts of Christian truth, but he also proposed that they were actually Christians!

> [Christ is the Word] of whom every race of men were partakers; and those who lived reasonably are Christians, even though they have been thought atheists; as, among the Greeks, Socrates and Heraclitus, and men like them; and among the barbarians, Abraham, and Ananias, and Azarias, and Misael,[22] and Elias, and many others whose actions and names we now decline to recount, because we know it would be tedious.[23]

Do you notice the remarkable claim made by Justin here? At first glance, it seems lightyears from the dark and pessimistic portrait of the religions we saw in Paul in the last chapter. But remember that Justin agrees with Paul that demons lurk behind most pagan religious ceremonies. And Paul himself seemed to see religious truth in the Greek poetry he quoted on Mars Hill.

But Justin goes beyond Paul by proposing that all poets and philosophers (and others, for that matter) who have religious truth not only got it from the Christ, but are actually followers of Christ—presumably, at least insofar as they practice such truth. Or, whether or not they follow Christ in a manner recognizable to later "Christians," they are counted as

---

[20] *Second Apology* 13.
[21] *Second Apology* 10.
[22] The last three are Greek names for Shadrach, Meshach and Abednego in Daniel 1:7.
[23] *First Apology* 46.

members of Christ's body by Justin. His evidence for such a revolution-
ary claim? Their tacit embrace of truths that Justin insists came only from
the Logos who is within every person. Most of them never heard of
Christ, but they have taken to be true those realities that came (without
their knowing it) from him, and they apparently have made those truths
central to their lives.

Part of the Logos versus All of the Logos

Before we conclude that Justin baptized his favorite Greek philosophers
as full-fledged Christian believers, let's take stock of what he did *not* say.
He did not say these philosophers had full knowledge of God through
Jesus Christ. That came only through *epignōsis,* "personal knowledge of
God," which came only through possession of the whole Logos, which
in turn is possible only through personal faith in Christ. Since that required conscious faith in Jesus of Nazareth as the Christ, pagans with no
knowledge of the gospel were out of luck, so to speak. They would
need to come into personal contact with Jesus Christ, which was possible (for those already dead such as Socrates and Plato) only through the
descent of Christ to the dead.[24]

So participation in part of the Logos was qualitatively different from
possession of the person of the Logos himself. As Justin put it, "The seed
and imitation imparted according to capacity is one thing, and quite another is the thing itself." The good pagan could be moral and know all
sorts of truth from the Christ. But he could never have the faith of the
Christian, which comes only from possession of the full Logos. Without
the latter, he could never "know God, the maker of all things through
Jesus the crucified." There were righteous pagans who, though uncir-
cumcised and failing to keep the sabbath, were yet "pleasing to God."
But they did not possess Christian *grace,* which is the presence of the
person of the Logos.[25]

Nor did Justin suggest that pagan religion is simply a different form

---

[24]Chrys Saldanha argues that Justin and other Fathers such as Clement of Alexandria believed
that the Christian tradition's stories of Christ's descent to the dead (Mt 27:52; 1 Pet 3:19; 4:6)
meant a postmortem opportunity for salvation for some, but only through personal and explicit
faith in Christ. Saldanha, *Divine Pedagogy: A Patristic View of Non-Christian Religions* (Rome:
Libreria Arteneo Salesiano, 1984), pp. 163-67.

[25]*Second Apology* 13; *Dialogue with Trypho* 34, 19, 92, 46.

of Christian religion. For Justin, Christian faith was unique, a new departure. The Greeks said Ultimate Reality lay beyond the world and would not enter it. But for Justin, only Christians knew that God came into the world, becoming man in Jesus Christ, dying on a cross and rising from the dead. For the Greeks, knowledge of God came from speculative investigation or observation of what could be seen, and then inferring the unseen from the seen. In contrast, Justin insisted that true knowledge of God was a relationship between God and the human person, possible only through personal knowledge of the God-become-man, Jesus Christ. Hence knowledge of God was not purely cognitive, providing new information *about* the divine, but union with God's very being. The gospel message was that God gave not just knowledge but his very self to humanity.

For Justin, then, there was both continuity and discontinuity between the pagan and Christian religions. Christ had sowed seeds of truth among the pagans. The Logos was actively present in every person. Therefore pagans could have real moral goodness and some genuine religious truth.

But the good pagan does not possess *epignosis,* personal knowledge of God. He does not lack faith and righteousness, but he does not have the faith and righteousness of the Christian stemming from union with God in Christ. He can be called a Christian because he has a sort of intermediate relationship to God, but he needs the gospel to have the fullness of relationship.

There is a link, then, between Christianity and the religions for Justin. But it is not a direct link. Hellenistic philosophy (which, you will recall, was as much religious as philosophical) could be a preparatory discipline leading to the perfection that comes only by personal and explicit knowledge of Jesus the Christ.

Why the Religions?

The central question of this book is, Why are there other religions? Or, to put it another way, What is the Father of Jesus Christ doing in the religions?

This was not the question that the early church in Justin's day had to confront. Instead, pagans challenged Christians with the question, If Christianity is true, why did it come so late in human history? Why is it so new? Today we tend to presume that what is new is better than the old. But in the ancient world, prestige always lay with what was more ancient. Christianity was a newcomer on the scene. Even if it was a child of Judaism, which could claim a hoary history, the central feature of this new brand of Judaism was the Christ, who had arrived just yesterday, so to speak.

Justin's answer was elegant. Christ has been in the world since its very beginning as the Logos. He has been in all human beings since the beginning, leading them to the truth and pulling them away from error. When the great thinkers of the past spoke truth, it was only because of Christ within them. The theophanies of the Old Testament were manifestations of the Christ; he spoke through the burning bush to Moses. The glories of Greece and Rome were inspired by Christ. Whatever evil has plagued the world has arisen and continued only because of human resistance to the truth and beauty of the Logos. Christ finally appeared in the flesh at the end of the ages to affirm the reality of the vision to which he had been pointing for all of history, and to die for the reconciliation of humanity with God.

Although our question was not Justin's main concern, his thinking about the religions gives us some helpful background. He said the pagan myths of his day were demonically inspired imitations and counterfeits, and that they arose from pride and the desire for power. Fallen angels lured human creatures away from the true god with manufactured rites and rituals, using fear and guilt to bind devotees to themselves. While Greek popular cults retained occasional glimmers of truth, Greek philosophy contained far more. Insofar as it was a response to the Logos, it was a gift of God, teaching a degree of Christian truth.

But if Justin helps us see connections between Christ and the religions, he does not directly address our principal concern: What could the Father of Jesus Christ be doing in these religions? Justin showed us that Jesus Christ was not completely absent from pagan religion, and he may in fact have been revealing a part of himself in and through them. But why did God permit all this? What was God's purpose in this partial revelation? And why was the vision of God so partial and incomplete?

Justin did not get that far. But Irenaeus and Clement of Alexandria thought they could answer these questions.

6

DIVINE PEDAGOGY

Irenaeus Explains How God Uses the Religions

"IN THE SUMMER OF 177 THERE TOOK PLACE AT LYONS one of the most terrible dramas in the history of the early Church."[1] The people and authorities of this city in Roman Gaul (now France) launched a persecution of Christians that has unnerved readers for nearly two millennia. Inspired by reports that believers were cannibals and libertines, first mobs and then the state subjected Christians to horrible torture and death.

The woman Blandina was the most famous. Her story and that of all the other martyrs of Lyons are preserved in an anonymous account handed down by a survivor to the church's first great historian, Eusebius. Blandina, he tells us,

> was filled with such power that those who took it in turns to subject her to every kind of torture from morning to night were exhausted by their efforts and confessed themselves beaten—they could think of nothing else to do to her. They were amazed that she was still breathing, for her whole body was mangled and her wounds gaped; they declared that torment of any one kind was enough to part soul and body, let alone a succession of torments of such extreme severity. But the blessed woman, wrestling magnificently, grew in strength as she proclaimed her faith, and found refreshment, rest, and insensibility to her sufferings in uttering the words, "I am a Christian: we do nothing to be ashamed of."[2]

The deacon Sanctus was also subjected to a string of horrific tortures,

---

[1]W. H. C. Frend, *Martyrdom and Persecution in the Early Church* (New York: New York University Press, 1967), p. 1.
[2]Eusebius *The History of the Church from Christ to Constantine* 5.1, trans. and intro. by G. A. Williamson (Harmondsworth, U.K.: Penguin, 1965).

but refused throughout to tell his name or race or birthplace or whether he was slave or free. To every question he replied in Latin, "I am a Christian." When the authorities could stand such defiance no more, they pressed red-hot copper plates against the most sensitive parts of his body. Again he was silent but for his simple self-identification. His whole body "was all one wound and bruise, bent up and robbed of outward human shape." But a few days later, when he was put on the rack, amazingly his body "became erect and straight." The rack proved to be "not punishment but cure."[3] He finally died, but only after demonstrating the power of God.

Biblis, a slave-girl who had earlier denied Christ under torture and accused Christians of crimes, changed her mind after seeing the courage of Blandina and others. She confessed Christ, and then, when on the rack herself, shouted out, "How could children be eaten by people who are not even allowed to eat the blood of brute beasts?"[4]

The bishop of the Lyons diocese, Pothinus, was over ninety years old. Scarcely able to breathe because of a lung ailment, the aged bishop was dragged by soldiers to the tribunal, accompanied by jeering crowds. When the governor asked him, "Who is the Christians' god?" Pothinus replied, "If you are a fit person, you will know." For that he was beaten with fists and feet, and thrown into prison where he died after two days.

Alexander was a physician noted for his love for God and boldness of speech. When the governor demanded to know who he was, and Alexander said simply, "A Christian," the governor was enraged. "Deliver him to the beasts!" he cried to his soldiers. But Alexander was tortured first. Among his torments was being seated in a red-hot iron chair. Even while his flesh was cooking, Alexander uttered not a sound but called out to the spectators, "Look! Eating men is what *you* are doing: *we* neither eat men nor indulge in any evil deeds." When he was asked for God's name, Alexander replied, "God hasn't a name like a man."

---

[3]Ibid.

[4]This and the following stories are found in Eusebius *History of the Church* 5.1-3. Biblis was referring to the early Christian observance of Jewish rules prohibiting blood remaining in meat after slaughter (Acts 15:20, 29).

The Missionary Bishop

There is reason to believe that this simple but powerful story of the Lyons martyrs was written by Irenaeus (c. 145-202), the bishop who was elected to succeed the martyred Pothinus. Somehow Irenaeus escaped arrest and survived this horrifying trial. Our best guess, based on the sketchy historical evidence that has survived, is that Irenaeus was on a journey to Rome when the persecution broke out.[5]

Irenaeus, who seems to have been raised in a Christian home, was a third-generation Christian teacher. He was a young disciple of the aged Polycarp (martyred in 155), who had been made bishop of Smyrna (on the west coast of what is now Turkey) by the apostle John. So Irenaeus was closely connected to the apostles.

While at Rome Irenaeus seems to have become a pupil of Justin, whom we saw in the last chapter. He quotes Justin and knows about the defection of one of Justin's students. He also shows sophisticated knowledge of Greek culture, referring to both Greek poets (Homer, Hesiod, Pindar, Sophocles) and philosophers (Plato, Pythagoras and Thales). But Irenaeus was less impressed by Greek philosophy than Justin. His theology was more thoroughly biblical. As one scholar has noted, there is "hardly an utterance of his on paganism that is not a quote from the Bible or a paraphrase of a biblical idea."[6]

Irenaeus was a missionary bishop, and it is in this capacity that he is of interest to us. Gregory of Tours, who was a historian of the Franks, tells us that through his teaching Irenaeus converted almost the whole city of Lyons and sent missionaries to other parts of France. Irenaeus's greatest concern was to show that apostolic Christianity was superior to its greatest religious rival, Gnosticism. (The word *Gnostic* comes from the Greek word *gnōsis,* for "knowledge." The Gnostics taught that salvation is from mystical knowledge rather than the work of Christ on the cross.)

---

[5]The most accessible sources in English on Irenaeus's life are Chrys Saldanha, *Divine Pedagogy: A Patristic View of Non-Christian Religions* (Rome: Libreria Arteneo Salesiano, 1984); and Joseph P. Smith, S.J., trans. and ed., *St. Irenaeus: Proof of the Apostolic Preaching* (New York: Newman Press, 1952), pp. 3-5.

[6]Saldanha, *Divine Pedagogy,* pp. 78-79.

The Gnostic Challenge

Gnostics taught that there are two gods. One is the supreme god, the invisible and incomprehensible Father who exists in the company of Aeons (divine beings) that were produced by emanation from the Father in a world called the Pleroma (lit. "fullness"). This Father is aloof from matter, which is evil and the product of a fallen Aeon. Our world was created or formed from chaotic matter by the second god, called the Demiurge, who was formed himself either by the supreme god (according to some Gnostics) or by the Aeons (according to others). This Demiurge lives in another world outside the Pleroma consisting of angels and human beings.

For the Gnostics, Christ was an Aeon who did not have a body, despite appearances to the contrary. He couldn't have had a body, they reasoned, because matter is evil and Christ was the good redeemer.

Gnostics taught that there are three kinds of human beings. First are the "spiritual ones" (*pneumatikoi* or πνευματικοί), who are the only people who can know and contemplate the supreme god, because only they have been given a revelation by Jesus Christ, who alone knows the Father. This means that before Jesus came to earth, the Father had been completely unknown to anyone—even the Aeons and the Demiurge. The second group are the "soulish" people (*psychikoi* or ψυχικοί), who have been given knowledge of the Demiurge by that god's special gift. These were the prophets and patriarchs of the Old Testament. Last are the "earthly" folks (*choikoi* or χοικοί), who, like the soulish ones, know only the Demiurge. But this last group knows only the Demiurge's created effects, not the god in himself.

The bottom line for our purposes is that for Gnosticism, which was Christianity's greatest rival in Irenaeus's day, pagans had no access whatsoever to the transcendent god. Christ, for Gnostics, was not fully God and was never known before the incarnation. And the creator of this world was an inferior and distasteful god who had created matter, which Gnostics believed to be evil. Both gods, then, seemed unjust. The Demiurge had created an evil world of matter, and the high god played favorites by revealing himself to only a select few. The latter was completely uninterested in and unrelated to human history.

The First Theology of History

Irenaeus's response was to develop what has been called the first Christian theology of history. He explained how God has been working through all of history to save a people for himself. In contrast to the Gnostic high god, who was uninterested in human life and experience, Irenaeus's God is not only interested enough to direct history but in fact enters the world of matter himself to restore relationships with humanity.

While the Gnostic supreme god gives the means to salvation to only a precious few, Irenaeus's God provides the means of salvation to all, because he wants all to be saved. Therefore he provides revelation of himself to all.

Irenaeus believed that all human beings on earth in his day had heard the gospel. He was wrong about that, but that is not significant for our purposes. We are concerned with the purpose of the religions, and therefore God's intentions for people who have not heard the gospel. What matters is what Irenaeus believed about people in previous eras who did not know the gospel and what he thought were God's plans for people throughout history. Knowledge of those things can tell us about his view of other religions and something about God's purposes in permitting a profusion of religions to rival the true religion of Christ.

The important thing at this point—especially in view of Gnosticism's position that pagans are completely in the dark about the true god—is Irenaeus's conviction that God has revealed himself to everyone throughout history. And not only has God revealed himself to all, but much of the revelation has come through the creation, which the Gnostics had written off as evil and completely unrelated to the high god.

The key to Irenaeus's position on revelation and creation is his insistence that Jesus Christ is directly related to the Creator, who is also the supreme God. The Gnostics had separated the good supreme god from the evil creator, and they said Jesus Christ was related only to the supreme god. Thus their system was dualistic, radically separating our lives and this world from the supreme God. But Irenaeus maintained that Jesus Christ is the Son of the supreme God, the very embodiment of the supreme God's essence. I use the word *embodiment* purposely, for Irenaeus overturned the Gnostic rejection of matter, teaching instead that Jesus was fully human in a real material body. By the incarnation, the supreme God showed that matter is good, not evil, and in fact can be indwelt by God himself.

Irenaeus also rejected the Gnostic teaching that Jesus had never been known before the first century. Jesus, he said, was cocreator with the Father and so was known through all the acts of creation (more on this shortly). Furthermore, Jesus was the manifest expression of God throughout the Old Testament. Since in all of those expressions Jesus was revealing the nature and identity of the Father, the Father had been made known since the creation to more than just a few "spiritual" ones. Revelation had been far more extensive than Gnostics allowed.

But Jesus was not only important because of his revelation of the Father. He was also the Savior. By his work, he opened the way for communion with the Father, so that human beings were able not only to know the nature of the supreme God, but also actually come into friendship and communion with him. This was Irenaeus's response, in brief, to the Gnostic heresy. You can see already that Irenaeus had some new ideas about God and religion—ideas that move beyond what we saw in Justin. But before we get to those and their implications for other religions, let's unpack Irenaeus's key ideas in a bit more detail. Then we will see the new light he shed on the religions.

God as Pedagogue

Irenaeus's grand metaphor was God as pedagogue. A pedagogue is a teacher who patiently leads his students step by step through a careful educational process. Irenaeus also presents God as a loving shepherd who created the world out of a desire to have a people to love and lead, as a shepherd loves and leads his flock. This shepherd is leading all of humanity through history towards its final goal—being remade into the image of his Son and coming into intimate friendship with himself.

So the divine shepherd is also a pedagogue who is teaching and training his flock through the course of history. He can teach only so much at a time, because he knows the limited capacities of his pupils. Irenaeus says that after the Fall we were infants as a race, needing discipline, capable of receiving only milk, not meat. This is why God revealed only a tiny part of his glory and saved the incarnation of his Son for many centuries later.[7] In his great treatise *Against Heresies,* Irenaeus wrote that humanity as a race was "a little one . . . a child" who had to "learn" how to love God.[8] He had to grow and become strong.

The human race was not only young and undisciplined. It had also allowed its heart to become hardened. Because of both "human infirmity" and "incontinence," God permitted the enactment of certain laws, such as the Old Testament laws allowing divorce (*AH* 4.15.2). Without these concessions to human weakness, too many would have turned away from God entirely.

The Ten Commandments were one stage in the divine pedagogy. They kept humans from idolatry, and trained them in what it means to "love [God] with the whole heart" (*AH* 4.15.2). This is why Christ was not revealed at the beginning—why the incarnation did not come for many centuries. Human beings weren't ready for it. It would have been incomprehensible, too much to bear. They would not have been prepared. Using Irenaeus's reasoning, we would say this is why we don't give a text on systematic theology to a new believer, or teach calculus to the arithmetic student. Irenaeus's point was that God planned a gradual course of preparation for his people to receive and understand the Incarnate Word. He prepared a long series of stages through history which eventually culminated in the supreme event. Without those stages of patient preparation, the final event would have been misunderstood. The student would neither have understood the advanced material nor been able to graduate into the real world of communion with God.

Even more remarkable, perhaps, is that the supreme event was a person, and this person was himself the one who was arranging history to prepare for his appearance. He was both advance man and featured candidate, both trainer for the race and the race itself. In other words, throughout history God was providing more and more understanding of himself, which would finally eventuate in the appearance of his Son; but the agent all the while of this divine self-communication was the Son

---

[7]Irenaeus *Against Heresies* 4.38.1-2, in *The Ante-Nicene Fathers,* ed. Alexander Roberts and James Donaldson, vol. 1 (Grand Rapids: Eerdmans/Edinburgh: T & T Clark, 1993).

[8]Irenaeus *Against Heresies* 4.15.2; *Proof of the Apostolic Preaching* 12. Hereinafter citations of *Against Heresies* (*AH*) will be given in parenthetical references in the text.

himself. As Irenaeus put it, "God cannot be known without God." We cannot see or know God unless God reveals himself to us. There is nothing in us naturally that enables us to know God. All true knowledge of him must come by God's initiative to reveal himself. And God has taken this initiative within his triune Self. The Father has chosen, from the very beginning of the creation, to reveal the divine being through the agent of the Son.

> For the Lord taught us that no man is capable of knowing God, unless he be taught of God; that is, that God cannot be known without God: but that this is the express will of the Father, that God should be known. For they shall know Him to whomsoever the Son has revealed Him. (AH 4.6.4)

Stages in Revelation

God the Son used different means at different stages to prepare for his coming. The first stage, according to Irenaeus, was the creation. Through the physical cosmos and the human person, the second person of the Trinity revealed the Father's presence and character. The world itself shows human beings that there was a Creator and Maker, and our own bodies and minds show us that there must have been an "Artificer" who formed us (AH 4.5.6).

The Son left his own imprint on the creation. The Son is God's Word, who is "inherent in the entire creation" (AH 2.6.1; 5.18.3). In his *Proof of the Apostolic Preaching,* Irenaeus writes,

> He is Himself the Word of God Almighty, Who in His invisible form pervades us universally in the whole world, and encompasses both its length and breadth and height and depth—for by God's Word everything is disposed and administered—the Son of God was crucified in these, imprinted in the form of a cross on the universe.[9]

This idea probably comes from Justin's influence on Irenaeus. Like Justin, Irenaeus saw the cross as a symbol of the unification of all human beings and all things in Christ. His outstretched arms on the cross seemed to beckon all to come to him and suggested the creation of all things by him—as his theological grandfather John had taught: "In the beginning was the Word. . . . All things came into being through him,

---

[9] *Proof of the Apostolic Preaching* 34.

and without him not one thing came into being" (Jn 1:1, 3). This is probably the origin of what has been called Irenaeus's "cosmic cross."

Justin had also spoken of the "implanted" Logos *(logos emphytos)* in every human person. The Latin version of Irenaeus's original Greek text—now lost—is *verbum infixus,* which is probably the Latin editor's rendering of *logos emphutos.* So while Justin saw the Word as seeds planted in every human person, Irenaeus pictured a Word that was embedded in the world and directing it to its proper end.

When Irenaeus says that the Word reveals God through the creation, he means that as a person looks at the creation and the ways in which it is maintained, the Word by impulse on the mind shows the person that this world must have had a maker, and that this maker was a divine father. Some non-Christians, he says,

> who were less addicted to [sensual] allurements and voluptuousness, and were not led away to such a degree of superstition with regard to idols, being moved, though but slightly, by His providence, were nevertheless convinced that they should call the Maker of this universe the Father, who exercises a providence over all things, and arranges the affairs of our world. (*AH* 3.25.1)

Irenaeus writes that the Word has also implanted in each mind the Decalogue—the content of the Ten Commandments. These were inscribed on every human heart, as Paul said in Romans 2:15, long before Moses was given the tablets by God. This "natural law" placed by the Word in every human mind was sufficient during the time of the Fathers (the Jewish patriarchs—Abraham, Isaac and Jacob), when at least some human beings followed this law in their hearts (*AH* 4.15.1-3).

So the Word has always acted, since the very beginning of the world, to reveal the true God to human beings. Not only is the Word imprinted in the very fabric of being, somehow showing the cross, but the Word also acts directly on the human mind as it experiences life, pointing the mind of every person to the Creator and Provider of all, and to the law which the Word has written on the heart. This is the first way in which God has always been revealing himself to every human being, through the creation—both the creation of the world and the creation of the human person—by the direct action of the Word.

Revelation Through the Jews

The second stage in God's unfolding revelation was the later history of the Jews. When the Jewish people started to abuse their liberty and refused to accept training through what God had taught the patriarchs, God found it necessary to "bridle" them with the "yoke of the Mosaic law" (*AH* 4.15). This law was given only after a rash of apostasies, which showed that the law inscribed on the heart, which had been sufficient for the patriarchs, was no longer sufficient for their descendants. To those who proved themselves "headstrong" and "unruly" in the desert after the Exodus, God "promulgated a law very suitable [to their condition]" (*AH* 4.14.2). Because "they turned themselves to make a calf . . . they were placed for the future in a state of servitude suited to their wish" (*AH* 4.15.1).

The Mosaic law was specially designed to get the Jews back on the right track. Besides specifying the content of the moral law—the Ten Commandments—it also contained rules for worship through the tabernacle and its sacrifices and legal strictures for the new Israelite desert nation. But these were not for all time and all places. They were designed specifically with these headstrong Jews in mind, at this particular time, and were intended to point to more important principles.

All these rules were "secondary" but intended to call the Jews to "primary" things; they were "typical" (from the Greek *typos*, "model," akin to "symbolic") and meant to represent "things that are real"; they were "temporal," "carnal" and "earthly," calling their users to what is "eternal," "spiritual" and "heavenly" (*AH* 4.14.3). In other words, the law with its hundreds of regulations was "adapted" to the Jews' "condition of servitude." Certain precepts were included only because of their "hardness of heart." Because of "human infirmity" and "incontinence," God permitted certain "indulgences" such as divorce, so that they would "not revert to idolatry, nor apostatize from God" (*AH* 4.15.1-2).

The purpose of the Law was not only to keep his people from apostatizing, but also to teach and train his people to "bear His Spirit and hold communion with God" (*AH* 4.14.2). In fact, Irenaeus said, Christ himself was speaking through Moses. So the Law itself was given through Christ. And when, in the later history of Israel, God raised up prophets, Christ was speaking through them too.

Recapitulation

The third stage in God's revelation of himself was the incarnation. In this stage, the emphasis was more on salvation. In other words, Christ was manifested in the flesh not only to show God but also to do the work of salvation. If God had only revealed himself, Irenaeus pointed out, we would not have been saved. That would have only revealed a world we could not enter. But in the incarnation, God provided a way to bring us into his very being.

God did this by what Irenaeus called "recapitulation." By this he meant that God started over again on the creation. God had intended for Adam and his progeny to have full communion with himself, which means sharing his nature. But the Fall destroyed that possibility. Sin significantly marred the divine image in humanity, and prevented the Father from being able to bring human beings into communion with himself. Therefore God made a fresh start in the incarnation. He reproduced the old creation but reversed the features of the Fall. He created the perfect man in Jesus, as it were. I say "as it were" because God did not create Jesus, since Christ always was, as the second person of the Trinity. But God united his Son with human nature in such a way that Jesus Christ was the perfect man that Adam was intended to be. Because Jesus was perfect, without sin, the Father could have communion with him. And because Jesus' human nature was *human*, like ours, *we* could have communion with God—because Jesus' human nature was the go-between that now linked us with God.

Irenaeus believed that nothing could be redeemed that was not assumed. In other words, Jesus had to take on whatever was fallen. So he took on human nature so that he could redeem it. He went through every condition of humankind so that he could redeem every condition. Since humans go from infancy to adulthood, Jesus went from infancy to adulthood. Since human beings endure pain and temptation to sin, Jesus felt pain and temptation to sin—and the latter of every sort (*AH* 2.22.4).

The result of this recapitulation was not merely the end of God's wrath toward humanity as a race, but readmission of a new redeemed race to the privileged position held by Adam as companion of God before the Fall. This meant both "a communion of God and man" and a new "incorruptibility" given to man.[10] No longer would people die forever. Now believers would be clothed with new life from above that would preserve them for eternity.

Universal Revelation

We can see, then, that Irenaeus believed that all human beings, from the beginning of the world, have been given revelation of God sufficient for salvation. Revelation has come in different ways and degrees, but every human being has seen enough of God to be able to believe and be saved by Christ.

What about those who came before Christ? This question was asked both by Irenaeus's fellow Christians and by the pagans to whom they were witnessing. Irenaeus's answer was that Christ the Word had revealed the Father through the Jewish prophets to the Jews, and through creation to the Gentiles. Both Jews and Gentiles therefore knew enough to be able to fear and love God and to "desire to see Christ" (AH 4.22.2). Even apart from seeing Christ, and in the case of the Gentiles, even without having the law of Moses, they were justified by faith:

> All the rest of the multitude of those righteous men who lived before Abraham, and of those patriarchs who preceded Moses, were justified independently of [requirements of the Jewish law], and without the law of Moses. (AH 4.16.2)

> [Christ came] for all men altogether, who from the beginning, according to their capacity, in their generation have both feared and loved God, and practiced justice and piety towards their neighbours, and have earnestly desired to see Christ, and to hear His voice. (AH 4.22.2)

Righteous Pagans

Irenaeus therefore believed in "righteous pagans" who by the Word were given light sufficient to hope for Christ. They "feared God and died in justice and had the Spirit of God within them, such as the patriarchs and the prophets and the just."[11] It was to both these pagans and also to believing Jews, who were "sleeping" in Hades before the incarnation,

---

[10] Proof of the Apostolic Preaching 6, 7.
[11] Proof of the Apostolic Preaching 56.

that Jesus came on Holy Saturday, the time between the crucifixion and resurrection. To these souls he preached the gospel, making plain what had to this point been revealed only in shadows and types (*AH* 4.22.2; 4.27.2; 5.31.1). To them all he gave the promise that they would be resurrected at his second coming, at the end of the world, to live on earth with him in bodily form—a new incarnation, as it were—for a thousand years (the "millennium"), and therefore would be able to live in the fullness of gospel truth. This would give them the same opportunity as the apostles enjoyed at Christ's first coming, to prepare for the vision of the Father in heaven (*AH* 5.32-35).

Irenaeus based his claim for postmortem gospel preaching in part on two biblical passages, both in 1 Peter, that have puzzled readers for thousands of years. In the first passage, Peter says Christ was "put to death in the flesh, but made alive in the spirit, in which also he went and made a proclamation [*ekēryxen,* the root of which is the most common New Testament word for 'preaching the gospel'] to the spirits in prison" (1 Pet 3:18-19). Just a few verses later he adds, "The gospel was proclaimed even to the dead, so that, though they had been judged in the flesh as everyone is judged, they might live in the spirit as God does" (1 Pet 4:6). For our purposes here it doesn't matter that biblical scholars are divided on the meaning of these cryptic statements. What does matter is that Irenaeus and other early interpreters saw in these passages the proclamation of the gospel to those who had not heard it during their time on earth.

Since, for Irenaeus, the revelation of God through the Son was given in different ways at different times, he believed the final judgment will take that into account. People will be judged on the basis of what they did with the revelation they received; God will not assume that all have received the same mode and degree of revelation. But Irenaeus did assume that all human beings had received some revelation of the Son of God the Savior—either through the revelation of the Son in creation, or at the time of the incarnation, or at some point after, through the preaching of the church. Those who did not know of the incarnation when they lived, but nevertheless lived in hope of something of the sort, will enjoy the second incarnation during the millennium, and respond in faith to the Son at that time. For that reason, no one will be saved without accepting the gospel of Jesus Christ. And none of the damned will be able to say they didn't know anything of the Son of God.

Sorting It Out

What does this mean for our questions about the religions? I think we can conclude three things. First, Irenaeus's theology of history was the first to suggest that God has always been at work in all the religions, working by the Word to move history toward its final culmination in Christ. This means that even the religions can be considered to be directed by God to help prepare the nations for the denouement in Christ.

This doesn't mean that Irenaeus spoke positively of other religions. In fact, he held a very negative view. The gods of the nations, he asserted, are not gods at all, but idols or demons. Paganism generally is a "religion of stones" (*AH* 4.7.2). It is not a legitimate road to salvation. If pagans are saved, it is only by a Word-illumined response to the creation. There is no revelation through the other religions themselves.

Yet at this point Irenaeus was innovative and suggestive. He clearly believed that righteous pagans who had not heard the gospel during their earthly lives could still be saved by explicit acceptance of the gospel—either in Hades on Holy Saturday or during the millennium. He believed everyone since the incarnation had heard the gospel and so had no need for these revelations after death. If he had in fact known of, say, Chinese people on the other side of the globe who had never heard the gospel, he might have extended this hope to them. They would be in the position of the righteous pagans before Christ.

But even if he would not have extended that hope to righteous pagans after Christ, we can learn from his conviction that there is no salvation apart from accepting the gospel, and that this can take place in ways beyond the earthly witness of the church. This clearly rules out salvation apart from Christ (a pagan who is saved because of his "righteous" response to God's revelation in nature, quite apart from the work of Christ on the cross), as well as the notion of "anonymous Christians" who are saved apart from any contact with the Christian gospel. Irenaeus, arguing from biblical data, insisted that there is no salvation apart from believing the gospel. On that his predecessors, and most Christians since, have agreed. But Irenaeus's novel move was to infer from some admittedly difficult passages the possibility of postmortem contact with the gospel. This demonstrates God's movement throughout history to reach all, to give the opportunity of salvation to all and to work "around" the religions, as it were, to present the gospel of his Son to all.

If the first lesson we can learn from Irenaeus is that God has been working through and "around" the religions since the beginning of history, the second lesson is that his work has been educative or pedagogical. God has been moving the human race steadily and progressively toward a final resolution in Christ. And every lesson in that long educational process has been taught by Christ himself. If Irenaeus himself did not talk about the religions as lessons in that education, we can say that the logic of his argument points in that direction. If God conceded some things to the Jews that were not his highest will because of their "infirmity," "incontinence" and "hardness of heart," perhaps there are things in the religions that reflect not God's highest will but accommodations to human weakness and obduracy. If God used preliminary stages to prepare the Jews for receiving their Messiah, perhaps God uses comparable stages in the religions to prepare pagans for the revelation of Christ. If God appointed rules that were temporary "instructions" for the Jews, perhaps some things in the religions are provisional preparations for more advanced lessons on the way to Christ.

But we need to be careful not to impose our own vision on Irenaeus. We cannot use Irenaeus to think of religions as seeds growing into a plant. Yet we can say that Irenaeus's vision of divine pedagogy permits us to think of the movement of souls from one religious vision to another by a "qualitative leap of transcendence."[12] That is, the Word may use not only creation but also limited truths in the religions themselves to create a yearning in hearts for the fulfillment of those truths, a fulfillment that comes with the preaching of the gospel.

Finally, we see a certain historical relativism in Irenaeus. Not that truth is relative for Irenaeus, for he was emphatic that the truth is absolute in the person of Jesus Christ. But God presents, by the Son, the truth of his Son in ways that are conditioned by historical circumstances. "By a great variety of ways, [God] led the human race to salvation. . . . the Word passing through all these men . . . drew up a code adapted to every con-

---

[12]Saldanha, *Divine Pedagogy*, p. 176.

dition of life" (*AH* 4.14.2). When the natural law implanted in human hearts failed to restrain people from idolatry, God turned to a written code. Later came the prophets, whose messages were first oral and then later put into writing. Only later did the Word become flesh, to instantiate what was previously shown in other ways. He instructed the Jews in the desert with a detailed sacrificial system, which was later eclipsed by the perfect sacrifice of the Son of God himself.

In other words, to a nation of slow learners, God used many different teaching methods over thousands of years to communicate the truth. It was the same truth, but it came through different methods and modes because of different hearts and capacities to learn. Since the word *relativism* suggests a diffidence about final truth that Irenaeus would disdain, perhaps a better word is *dispensationalism*. Irenaeus saw God revealing his three persons and ways differently, depending on the historical dispensation. This does not mean, of course, that Irenaeus taught what goes by the name today of "conservative Protestant dispensationalism," which highlights the endtimes and owes more to C. I. Scofield than to St. Paul. But Irenaeus did believe that God varied the content of faith (while keeping the way of salvation uniform) according to the content of revelation given in each historical period.

Irenaeus would never have conceded that pagans learn the same truths through their religions as Christians learn through the gospel. For he insisted that no one can be saved except through the gospel. And if anyone is saved, it is only by what the gospel proclaims—the death and resurrection of Christ. This is true for both those who hear and those who don't hear the gospel in this life.

What Irenaeus suggests, however, is that God has not worked in the same ways with all people. God saves through the Word, his Son. But the way in which he joins people to the Son and his cross, so that he can bring them with him to the Father, has varied over time. According to Irenaeus, it has always involved believing the gospel. But that believing has come under different circumstances, in different ways and at different times in relation to one's death. This historical dispensationalism, rooted in the absolute truth of salvation only by Jesus Christ, demonstrates God's historical creativity. As the writer of the letter to the Hebrews put it, "Long ago God spoke to our ancestors *in many and vari-*

ous ways by the prophets" (Heb 1:1, emphasis added).

As we will see in the chapters to come, other Christian thinkers have picked up where Irenaeus left off on this subject of divine creativity. Clement of Alexandria, for example, concluded that God used the Greek religions as a separate covenant for the Gentiles. To him we now turn.

7

A Divine Gift to the Greeks

Clement of Alexandria and
the Gentile Covenants

THE CHURCH IN ALEXANDRIA AT THE END of the second century was facing a difficult choice. Educated Christians felt they had to choose between their heads and their hearts. Their surrounding culture was buzzing with heresies that were cleverly defended with sophisticated philosophy, while most Christians hid behind a narrow orthodoxy that tended to be anti-intellectual.

Alexandria was the second city of the empire, with a half million inhabitants. A bustling center of trade, commerce and culture, its museum and adjacent library attracted scholars, adventurers and charlatans from around the Mediterranean and beyond. Christians had been in Alexandria for nearly one hundred and fifty years. The fourth-century historian Eusebius tells us that Mark (Paul's companion and probable author of the gospel) was Alexandria's first bishop. This is plausible, since Luke reports that Apollos, a native of Alexandria, may have learned about Jesus in Alexandria before he met Aquila and Priscilla (Acts 18:24-26).

But ordinary Christians had come to fear any Christianity that claimed philosophical support. They had seen Gnostics use Scripture and philosophy to promote hedonism and ridicule the Old Testament. This prompted Tertullian to write, "Philosophy is the mother of all heresy." The heretics, he added, quote "Seek and you shall find" (Mt 7:7) to defend their speculations. But for Tertullian, "After one has believed, there is but one more thing to be believed—namely, that there is nothing more to believe."[1]

---

[1]Tertullian *Prescription Against Heretics* 9.

Christians came to believe that, like Odysseus's companions passing the sirens, they needed to stop up their ears lest they never return home. Ordinary disciples became convinced they should study only the basic teachings of the faith. Philosophy would only distract and would be of no use to reach their final goal—union with God in heaven. Many believed philosophy was invented by the devil to keep human beings from the final truth.

Pagan intellectuals had taken note. Celsus, writing in the same period and possibly from Alexandria, observed that while some Christians were educated, most usually told one another, "Don't ask questions, just believe. Faith will save you. Wisdom is an evil thing, and foolishness good."[2] Galen, the ancient medical authority who was a contemporary of Clement, remarked cynically, "If I had in mind people who taught their pupils in the same way as the followers of Moses and Christ teach theirs—for they order them to accept everything on faith—I should not have given you a definition."[3]

Clement of Alexandria, a Christian scholar who taught at a Christian academy there, realized this was a pastoral crisis. Seekers needed to know that they didn't have to cut off their heads to study the Christian faith. Believers needed to know that questions about faith are legitimate and that their faith could hold its own intellectually against all comers. Too many seekers and believers had concluded that faith had nothing to do with reason. Or that they had to dismiss all philosophy and other religions as completely devoid of truth.

Clement spent most of his career arguing that wherever truth and reason are found, Logos had already visited. "The earth is the LORD's and all that is in it" (Ps 24:1), he kept repeating. All truth found in the vast array of the human sciences is from God. Rather than undermining Christian truth, these other kinds of truth actually reinforce it. Clement insisted that Christians should not be afraid of philosophy, for it contains truth useful for leading seekers to the full truth. It is a kind of preparatory training that helps make people virtuous, which in turn helps them receive further truth. Clement likened philosophy to plowing the ground so that it can

---

[2]Origen *Against Celsus* 1.9.
[3]Richard Walzer, *Galen on Jews and Christians* (London: Oxford University Press, 1949), pp. 15, 48-56.

then receive spiritual seed. Philosophy, he said, helps purge the soul from obsession with material things; it teaches the mind to regard things that cannot be seen. It leads the soul from meditation on the visible and created to contemplation of the invisible and uncreated.[4]

In fact, said Clement, philosophy is a gift of God. It came originally from the fallen angels of Genesis 6, who imparted their secrets to women. While their secrets are distortions of the truth, kernels of truth nonetheless remain. As long as we recognize that philosophy is a harlot (Prov 5:20) and are careful not to linger too long with her, we can use her to help instruct seekers and young believers. We can use it to lead their minds beyond it, showing them that the truth amidst the distortions leads to the fuller Truth who walked among women and men.

Clement in Hellenistic Alexandria

Clement (c. 150–c. 215) was probably born in the mid-second century in Athens, where he was educated as a pagan. He seems to have been initiated into the mysteries of Eleusis, a Greek religion involving shouted obscenities, a special barley drink, and symbolic dying and rebirth. At some point, while he was still in Athens, Clement converted to faith in Christ. Like many in that era wanting to pursue truth, he traveled in search of teachers, going to Italy, Syria, Palestine, Egypt and eventually Alexandria. He finally settled in Alexandria because of Pantanaeus, a Christian teacher whom Clement called a "truly Sicilian bee," which means, since the best honey came from Sicily, that Clement considered him the brightest teacher of all.

Alexandria was not only a commercial center of the Roman Empire, but also a cultural mecca, attracting sorcerers, magicians, philosophers from schools both East and West, astrologers, Gnostics, Christians, and Jews. Into this religious and philosophical melting pot came young educated Greeks, looking for spiritual direction. Most assumed that *aretē* (moral virtue) was a necessary prerequisite to finding God. They sought out philosophers for moral and spiritual direction to teach them how to control their passions and mind. Only a purified mind, it was

---

[4]Clement *Stromata, or Miscellanies* 1.5, 1.13-17, 77 passim, in *The Ante-Nicene Fathers,* ed. Alexander Roberts and James Donaldson, vol. 2 (Peabody, Mass.: Hendrickson, 1994).

believed, was able to see God.

In this atmosphere, where "philosophy" was part and parcel of a religious quest, Clement proclaimed that Christian faith was "the true philosophy," "philosophy according to Christ," "the wisdom of God," "the only authentic and unassailable truth in which we are instructed by the Son of God."

A Work of Divine Providence

But first Clement had to persuade his fellow Christians that philosophy was worthy of study. It is, he argued, because it is from God. In fact, it is a "divine gift to the Greeks." Against those Christians who complained that philosophy was a waste of time or even evil, Clement insisted it "is in a sense a work of divine Providence."[5]

Greek philosophy (which, as I have argued in previous chapters, was as much religious as philosophical because it was an all-encompassing approach to ultimate reality) was not an unmixed blessing, however. Clement taught that it contained untruth as well as truth. This was due to its origin in theft. At this point, Clement drew upon the *prisca theologia* tradition, which we have seen in Justin Martyr, and also the fallen angel motif that goes back to the Old Testament. He believed that the fallen angels, which "are distributed over the nations and cities,"[6] stole portions of God's truth and inspired the Greek philosophers with it, scattering among them the seeds of the truth they had pilfered. Because the angels had rebelled against God and served the devil, they mixed deception with verity.

But Clement responded that even if the devil's minions pulled this off, God nevertheless permitted it, so it was ultimately a work of divine providence. Thus, if some Christians charged truth in Greek philosophy to a kind of accident, Clement replied that it was still part of a divine plan. If it could be called good fortune that philosophy replicated some biblical truth, Clement's retort was that it was not unforeseen. Or, if some said the Greeks perceived truth by their own nature, Clement hastened to add that God created their nature, and gave them a "spirit of perception."[7]

---

[5]Clement *Stromata* 1.1.
[6]Clement *Stromata* 6.17.
[7]Clement *Stromata* 1.19; 6.17.

Partial Truth

So the pagans have some truth. Drawing no doubt on John 1:9, Clement argued that, to some extent, all the Greek philosophers were "illumined by the dawn of light."[8] He compared the Hellenic philosophers to a nut with a shell that must be cracked and opened to get at the kernel within. The kernel is edible and therefore useful. But it is not the same as more substantial food such as meat.

The Hellenic kernel is partial truth, while the Christian philosophy is Truth itself. The Greek thinkers know things of this world, but Christians see spiritual things beyond this world. The philosophers have "rudimentary" knowledge; Christians have "perfect" knowledge. The former have the "names," while the latter possess the "things" themselves. Other philosophies and religions declare things "about" God, but Christians "declare God." The philosophers have the faint light of a wick; Christians have the sun. Greeks know the "accidents" (an Aristotelian word for qualities not essential to a thing), but Christians know "the essence." They speak of and guess at the truth, but we, said Clement, apprehend the Truth and know that "the Truth interprets itself." Philosophers name God; Christians know God. They seek the probable; Christians see the True. They search; we find. Theirs is a "searching," ours the "finding." They are limited in the "extent of knowledge [and] proof that is really authoritative," but "we are taught of God, being instructed in the truly 'sacred letters' by the Son of God."[9]

The Greek Covenant

For Clement, then, non-Christians have truth that is partial. But it is not only partial. It is also of a different quality from Christian truth. There is truth in geometry that is of a special kind. The same can be said for music. Each has its own kind of truth. But Christian truth is not just a skill or discipline, as in geometry and music. It is also personal knowledge— not just knowing about Jesus Christ, but knowing him. Its truth is received in faith, which is the response of the whole person—body, mind

---

[8]Clement *Stromata* 1.13.
[9]Clement *Stromata* passim. This compilation of comparisons in Clement is drawn from Saldanha, *Divine Pedagogy,* pp. 119-20. I owe much of my understanding of Clement to Saldanha's insightful analysis.

and soul. So Christian truth is the only complete truth, in relation to which all other truths are partial and analogical. Other truths pertain to only one part of the person, but Christian truth engages every part of the person. And it is comprehensive, which means that every other kind of truth is illumined by its light.

Did the Greek philosophers know and worship the same God whom Christians know and worship? Clement said *yes and no*. Yes, they knew the true God, but dimly. They were unbelievers, deserving of God's judgment and condemnation if they persisted in unbelief when once they are shown the truth. But most pagans have some faint knowledge of the Creator of all things:

> For there was always a natural manifestation of the one Almighty God, among all right-thinking men; and the most, who had not quite divested themselves of shame with respect to the truth, apprehended the eternal beneficence in divine providence. . . . Far from destitute of a divine idea is man, who, it is written in Genesis, partook of inspiration, being endowed with a purer essence than the other animate creatures.[10]

And of all the pagans, the Greeks were among the best, at least in regard to their knowledge of God. They erred plenty, but unlike most races, they suspected that polytheism was wrong, "which suspicion is no insignificant seed, enabling the germ of good sense to grow into truth."[11]

In fact, God gave philosophy to the Greeks in much the same way that he gave the law to the Jews—to prepare them for the further revelation of his Christ—"to fit their ears for the Gospel."[12] In each case, it was a covenant—a unilateral gift by God to train a people for further revelation and closer relationship to himself.

> The same God that finished both the Covenants was the giver of Greek philosophy to the Greeks, by which the Almighty is glorified among the Greeks. . . . From the Hellenic training, and also from that of the law, are gathered into the one race of the saved people those who accept faith: not that the three peoples [Jews, Christians and Greeks] are separated by time, so that one might suppose three natures, but trained in different

---

[10]Clement *Stromata* 5.14.
[11]Clement, *Protreptikos*, or *An Exhortation to the Greeks* 2.42.2 in *Clement of Alexandria*, trans. G. W. Butterworth (Cambridge, Mass.: Harvard University Press, 1960).
[12]Clement *Stromata* 6.6.

Covenants of the one Lord, by the word of the one Lord. For that, as God wished to save the Jews by giving to them prophets, so also by raising up prophets of their own in their own tongue, as they were able to receive God's beneficence, He distinguished the most excellent of the Greeks from the common herd.[13]

Intriguingly, then, God gave prophets to the Greeks. While they were given wisdom from God, their wisdom was miniscule in comparison to what God gave to the Jewish prophets. In comparison to the "organs of the divine voice" in Scripture, the Greek prophets were false prophets. Not false in all substance, but so disproportionately pinched in their vision of the Light that their vision was darkness compared to the Sun of truth in the Bible. Clement wrote of Homer's "theology," Greek "theologizing" and Orpheus the "theologian," but by those terms he meant simply that they were dealing with questions about God. He conceded that because of the Greek covenant there was a certain "divination" among the Greeks, but it was little more than guesswork. They had truth, but it was mixed with error—unlike the purity of truth in the Scriptures.

Not Essential for Faith

Therefore Greek philosophy, despite its ultimate provenance in God and its admixture of truth, is finally not essential for faith. Most Christians in fact have never read it or learned from it. It is one of many secondary approaches to the truth that God has established. God is the cause of all things, but of some things principally and of other things secondarily. The way of faith through Christ is the principal way to God that he has established, and it is for all human beings. But there are many secondary approaches to this primary way. God has caused even these secondary approaches, and Greek philosophy is one of them. Each of these secondary approaches is meant to lead to the primary way of faith through Christ. The secondary approaches are starting points and preparatory trainings intended to lead people to faith in Christ. They are ways *to* salvation, not ways *of* salvation: "Philosophy therefore was a preparation, paving the way for him who is perfected in Christ."[14]

---

[13]Clement *Stromata* 6.5.

[14]Clement *Stromata* 1.5.

Since Greek philosophy is a secondary approach, just as the Jewish law was a secondary approach to the primary path of faith in Christ, each provides a kind of righteousness that is insufficient for salvation. Both the Jewish law and Greek philosophy confer a righteousness based on fear rather than love.[15] This is a good preliminary stage, but Jesus said it is not enough: "Unless your righteousness exceeds that of the scribes and Pharisees, you will never enter the kingdom of heaven" (Mt 5:20). Even those who are righteous by virtue of their participation in the Law or Greek wisdom need faith in Christ.

Heathen in Hades

This is why, Clement argues, Christ descended to Hades in what has been called by tradition "the harrowing of hell." He went to give a chance for salvation to those who had not heard the gospel while they were on earth. Clement refers to those who lived before the first century, when Christ appeared, and in lands outside Palestine, where the Jewish law was not known (like Irenaeus, he seems to have assumed that everyone who was living in his own century had a chance to hear the gospel). He says that Jesus and even the apostles went to Hades (he intimates that there are different degrees of retributions, and thus presumably this is different from hell, where the most serious offenders would be punished) to preach the gospel to those who never had the opportunity to hear it on earth.

> For it is not right that these should be condemned without trial, and that those alone who lived after the advent should have the advantage of the divine righteousness [that comes by faith in Christ]. But to all rational souls it was said from above, "Whatever one of you has done in ignorance, without clearly knowing God, if, on becoming conscious, he repent, all his sins will be forgiven him.[16]

So Christ and "the apostles also, as here [on earth], so there [in Hades] preached the Gospel to those of the heathen who were ready for conversion."[17] "It is evident," he concludes, that some of these heathen in

---

[15]Clement *Stromata* 7.12.
[16]Clement *Stromata* 6.6.
[17]Clement *Stromata* 6.6.

Hades "who were outside the Law, having lived rightly . . . on hearing the voice of the Lord, whether that of His own person or that acting through His apostles, with all speed turned and believed."[18]

Salvation, then, comes only through preaching the gospel. There are different means of preparation, by different covenants, and so God works in different ways to reach different peoples and cultures. But all these diverse streams must eventually join the same river which proceeds to God only by passing through knowledge of Christ by gospel preaching.

Therefore philosophy is of only limited use. Christian "Gnostics" (for Clement, these are mature Christians trained in the Scriptures) should not revert to philosophy for their understanding of truth, since Greek philosophy is meant to lead one to the truth of the Scriptures. They will not turn to Plato and Aristotle as their principal source of understanding; instead they will see them as secondary and to be used only for particular situations. Christian faith gained through the Bible is bread or true food; Greek philosophy is merely sauce or dessert.

Three Uses

Clement identified three uses for Greek philosophy. First, he said, it is a didactic aid. It should be used to help teach young Christians trying to learn the faith. Those who have been steeped in Greek literature will need Christian teachers who are able to interpret Greek thinking from a Christian perspective. They can show their students how the Greeks asked questions that Christ answers, or how Greek thinkers outlined shadows that are fully illumined by Christ.

Second, Greek philosophy is useful for apologetics. Christian teachers can use it to help resist attacks from sophists, pagan critics who were interested only in denouncing Christian faith as anti-intellectual. Hence Greek thought can be used as a "hedge and wall of the vineyard" to protect the faith from scurrilous attacks.[19] These apologetic defenses were aimed not at the sophists themselves, whom Clement knew would never be persuaded to change their minds, but at Christians who feared that

---

[18]Clement *Stromata* 6.6.
[19]Clement *Stromata* 1.20.

faith was not up to intellectual challenge. They would also show Christians a way beyond naive interpretations of the Bible that only provided fodder for sophist charges of irrationality.

Third, Greek philosophy could be profitable for *gnosis*. In other words, it could help demonstrate the beauty of orthodox theology by perfecting systematic understanding of the faith. This doesn't mean that the Greek thinkers could contribute much to an informed Christian's understanding of God. But it could help her make connections among various elements of the truth revealed in the Scriptures. It's like the wild olive tree that absorbs lots of food and water through the soil but produces no fruit. Not until it is grafted into a cultivated tree does fruit appear. So too, philosophy can help produce fruitful knowledge of truth, but only when grafted onto the Word.

Why the Religions?

Now that we have reviewed Clement's general approach to the dominant religion of his culture, which he called "Greek philosophy," we are prepared to get at Clement's answers to the question that dominates this book, Why are there religions at all? Or more specifically, Why did God allow other religions besides the true one, Christian faith?

Clement first discusses the reason for religious differences at all. He says they are rooted in differences of disposition. God, he writes, "called all equally." But his gifts were distributed unequally "in proportion to the adaptation possessed by each." Some were apparently eager to take in all he could give. These Clement calls "Gnostics"—to be distinguished from the heretics of his day who went by the same name. Clement's point in using the same word, which means "possessor of knowledge," is that only learned Christians have true knowledge.[20]

Others embrace truth from God, but for various reasons are able to take in only so much. These are "believers." Still others are "hard of heart." God is the teacher of all three of these groups. The first group are his friends, the second "faithful servants," and the third his "servants merely." The first he trains by mysteries, the second "by good hopes," and the third "by corrective discipline."

---

[20]All of the quotations in this and the following paragraphs come from *Stromata* 7.2.

Because of God's knowledge of the different "adaptations" to his more general revelations in nature and conscience, God gave the Law to the Jews and philosophy to the Greeks. God's giving the Law to the Jews did not mean, however, that the Jews were more righteous: "For the law is not appointed for a righteous man." But for some other reasons, which Clement apparently did not know, God "shut up" both peoples to "unbelief" before the incarnation in the first century.

Then Clement detailed, in good David Hume[21] fashion, stages in the history of religions. Originally, he said, there was an innate communion of human beings with God, which after a time became obscured through ignorance.[22] Humans took their relationship with God for granted and failed to pass down through the generations the original understanding of God and how to maintain that communion.

But God was not ready to give up on his human creatures. He knew from the beginning that this backsliding would take place. So, according to a predetermined plan, and because he did not want the race to depart from him completely and thereby perish, he permitted men and women to worship the elements (the sun, moon and stars). Seen from below, humans were simply turning away from the heavenly orientation with which they were created, to obsession with the earth in which they had been placed. But God knew all about this, and decided to use this "fall" from original intentions to worship of the elements, to induce them to eventually rise up to worship the Creator of the elements. So even the next phase in the history of the religions—worship of nature—was superintended by God and coopted to serve his larger redemptive designs.[23]

The next stage was even further declension—from worship of the elements themselves to worship of images of them. They "would not abide by those heavenly bodies assigned to them, but fell away from them to stocks and stones."[24] The Scythians started to worship sabers, the Arabs stones, and the Persians rivers. Other races worshiped blocks of wood or pillars of stone.[25]

---

[21]The British philosopher whose *Dialogues Concerning Natural Religion* (1750s) famously proposed that religion evolved in discrete stages, with polytheism preceding monotheism.

[22]Clement *Protreptikos* 2, p. 51.

[23]Clement *Stromata* 6.14; *Protreptikos* 2, pp. 51-55.

[24]Clement *Stromata* 6.14.

[25]Clement *Protreptikos* 4.

Then came the last stage, euhemerism, or worship of human beings turned into gods. The objects of wood and stone took on human shapes, and these became the idols which the Greeks came to worship.[26] Because Clement believed the Greek gods were once men whom "fable and time have raised . . . to honor," he mocked their inane and immoral antics. In his *Protreptikos,* or *Exhortation to the Heathen,* Clement went to great lengths trying to demonstrate that Greek myths were both illogical and absurd. But Clement was hardly alone in his interpretation of the religions. The notion that a human being might become a god or daemon after death was commonly held in his day.[27]

What Can We Learn?

Clement's massive reflections on the religions of his day give us plenty to think about[28]—particularly when we recall that Greek philosophy was what we would call today both philosophy of religion and religion itself. Plato and Aristotle wrote not only about the meanings of words but the meaning of the cosmos—not only about things, but also about God and his relation to all things in the cosmos. Not only about what is, but how we ought to live in the face of what is. So when Clement writes about Greek philosophy, we should think of what we call religion—an overarching conception of the origin and meaning of everything that exists. Clement distinguished Greek mythology (stories about Greek gods and goddesses) from Greek philosophy (which tended toward monotheism). But by "Greek philosophy" he nevertheless meant a way of viewing the world that sought to explain all that is and to teach us how, as a result, we should live and think.

Hence when Clement tells us that Greek philosophy contains both truth and error, we would not be remiss in extending that consideration to the great world religions we know today. They too contain both truth and error. But, if we are to learn from Clement, we would understand that that mixture of truth and error is there by divine design. It is not

---

[26]Ibid. 4.

[27]Marcus Dodds, *Pagan and Christian in an Age of Anxiety* (Cambridge: Cambridge University Press, 1965), p. 74.

[28]The great fifth-century biblical scholar Jerome said Clement was the most learned of the Fathers; *Epistulae* 70.4. His enormous collection of theological reflection shows prodigious knowledge of ancient pagan thinking.

there by accident or simply good fortune. Neither does truth exist in the religions merely because certain non-Christians possessed extraordinary spiritual insight. Clement would insist that God is the ultimate cause of all, and therefore that insight was given to those non-Christian thinkers by God.

At the same time, Clement would tell us, there is a difference between truth in the religions and truth in the full glare of light from the Son of God. The religions teach a knowledge obtained from afar, while the Son of God gives us direct and personal knowledge of the Trinity. Knowledge of God in the religions is of a different quality, and only partial, when compared to the fullness of revelation provided by the Christ.

Many of the religions, Clement would say, worship the same God whom Christians worship. For there is indeed only one God. Therefore to the extent that the religions apprehend truly that God, beside whom there is no other, they have seen and worshiped the true God. But when contrasted with apprehension of God accessible to Christians, the religions' knowledge is only dim and faint.

Nevertheless, God may have given other religions as covenants of sorts to certain peoples, much as he gave Greek philosophy to the Greeks, to prepare them to receive the gospel. The religions may even have their own prophets who were taught by God, similar to the Greek thinkers whom Clement called "prophets." Yet the prophets of the religions differ qualitatively from the Hebrew prophets through whom the Holy Spirit speaks in the Scriptures. Pagan prophets reflect in broken and pale light truths given by God, while the biblical prophets wrote with the blazing light of direct revelation. Pagan prophets' writings are mixtures of truth and error, but the biblical prophets give us the unvarnished truth of God. Therefore, while Clement uses the same word, *prophets,* for these two groups of seers, one group is clearly in a class by itself.

Hence knowledge of the religions is unnecessary for every Christian believer. The religions were given by God in a secondary way: they were *permitted* by God to certain peoples for particular times and obscure reasons related to their "adaptations" and God's inscrutable purposes. Even if God permitted them for limited purposes, they are still filled with much error alongside whatever truth they may have. This is why they were usually limited to a particular people for a limited time. But Christian faith was given *directly* and in *primary* manner to the world, and it was intended to be received eventually by every people.

Therefore Christian faith is necessary to every people and person for salvation. The story of Christ and the apostles going to Hades is a symbol of this need—that faith in God under other names in the religions is not enough. That faith must eventually be replaced by faith in Jesus Christ through the preaching of the gospel, which will be provided in some time and manner even if not visibly in this life.

Hence there are three uses for the religions in the life of the church. The first is didactic. For those seekers who are coming out of other religions and for young converts who also were raised in the religions, it is helpful and perhaps necessary for church teachers to be able to relate Christian teaching to the teaching of other religions. Christian teachers should be able to show both how Christ fulfills the promises made by the religions and to correct false images of God and salvation taught by the religions.

Second, knowledge of the religions is helpful for apologetics, which is useful more for Christians than unbelievers. Christians more and more are asking how Christ relates to the Buddha and to Allah (and of course other gods/religions). Only teachers who know the religions will be able to show the important connections and distinctions which need to be made. Otherwise it will be easy for some Christians to conclude that Christ may be just one more manifestation of God, each of which is relatively equal in truth.

Third, the religions can help theologians perfect their understanding of the faith. It is the job of systematic theology to relate Christian faith to every human enterprise. As the role of the religions becomes increasingly visible in geopolitics and crosscultural relations, theologians can demonstrate in fresh ways how Christian faith answers or at least confronts the questions that other gods and faiths raise. In addition, conflicts between the religions and Christian faith can help uncover more of the meaning of Jesus Christ—just as interreligious encounter has expanded Christian understanding for two millennia. One example of this was the early church's use of Greek philosophy of religion to help explicate the Trinity.[29]

Finally, Clement helps Christians understand why there are other religions. He tells us that part of the answer lies in different dispositional responses to God's original revelations of himself. We can learn from Clement that God cares for all and works in all cultures and persons to draw them to himself, with the goal of reconciling all the world to himself. Clement suggests that God permitted other, partially false religions in order to keep some peoples from complete destruction. Their religions gave them a measure of truth, enough to keep them in some contact with God. The divine plan was to use these religions as way stations from which to eventually bring them to fuller truth.

Clement's suggestions are both helpful and problematic. They open up a useful line of thinking about God's original and then provisional purposes: an original purpose of giving the full truth to all, but then the provision of partial truths to those who would not receive the fuller version. This is similar to the broader biblical story of Fall and redemption—that originally eternal life was provided for the human race in the garden, but that sin required a new plan of redemption to unfold (Gen 2—3; Rom 1—6).

But the problem comes when we consider Clement's proposal that some peoples were more receptive than others, and that these peoples were identified with different religions. Christians, then, would have reason to boast that they were more receptive and therefore more righteous than Muslims or Buddhists. Yet the biblical testimony is that no human being or society is receptive to God, "there is no one who seeks God" (Rom 3:11). Salvation does not come because of what we do, "so that no one can boast" (Eph 2:9).

Clement acknowledges that the law was not given as a reward for righteousness; quite the contrary, it was given to lawbreakers. But the notion of merit subtly remains—the hint that Christians and Christian societies were somehow more receptive and on that basis were given Christian revelation—while Muslims growing up in Muslim nations must not have been as receptive to God's original revelation. Christians com-

---

[29]See H. E. W. Turner, *The Pattern of Christian Truth: A Study in the Relations Between Orthodoxy and Heresy in the Early Church* (Eugene, Ore.: Wipf and Stock, 2004).

mitted to the biblical understanding of salvation cannot accept this.

Perhaps we can learn from Clement that receptivity and its absence might explain something of the origins of some of the religions—and thus perhaps why God permitted these religions in the first place. That is, perhaps the near-universal response to God's full revelation was rejection or indifference. This seems to be the balance of the biblical perspective. Perhaps in response, as humans created alternative religions, God sprinkled some of his truth to save them from utter destruction—or, as Clement and other early thinkers put it, God permitted fallen angels to distribute their distorted versions of truth.

But we must also be silent where Clement is silent, acknowledging by that silence that we simply know no more. This last conjecture is exactly that—conjecture based on thin lines of biblical evidence. Moreover, we cannot say anything about the receptivity of the millions of believers in other religions today, particularly those who have not understood with clarity the Christian gospel.

8

DIVERSE DESTINIES
BY DIVERSE CHOICES

Origen's Warnings About Other Religions

SOMETIME AFTER 222 C.E., A YOUNG CHRISTIAN THINKER named Origen 185-253 (C.E.), living in Caesarea, the port of Palestine, was summoned by the emperor's mother to Antioch in Syria. Julia Mamaea, whose son was Alexander Severus (emperor from 222 to 235), was "a religious woman if there ever was one."[1] She had undergone initiation rites into the cults of many different divinities, and now wanted to hear about a new deity named Jesus. Her own son, the emperor, prayed every morning before images of Orpheus, Apollonius of Tyana[2] and Jesus. Julia had no intention of making Jesus her only god. But like most people in her period, she believed that each god represented a different aspect of the Divine. To be truly spiritual, it was thought best to become initiated into as many deities as possible.

Julia Mamaea's passion for religion was not unusual in the third-century pagan world of the eastern Mediterranean. The Olympian gods associated with the city-state and its familial values had been around for centuries. The gods of nature and the underworld, such as Demeter,

---

[1]Eusebius *The History of the Church from Christ to Constantine* 6.21, trans. and intro. by G. A. Williamson (Harmondsworth, U.K.: Penguin, 1965).

[2]Orpheus was a legendary Greek poet from Thrace, whose devotees often used asceticism (deprivation of the comforts of the flesh) to try to achieve reunion with the divine "One." Apollonius was a first-century C.E. itinerant sage who was believed to have healed the sick, cast out demons and ascended to heaven after death. For more on these and other elements of Hellenistic religion, see Luther H. Martin, *Hellenistic Religions: An Introduction* (New York: Oxford University Press, 1987).

goddess of grain, and Dionysus, god of wine and spirit, had become popular since the death of Alexander the Great in the third century B.C.E. Perhaps because of the influence of Stoicism,[3] many had come to see the gods as allegorical expressions of a single, universal, divine reality—logos. More recently, Egyptian religions focusing on the nature deities Isis and Osiris had spread around the Mediterranean. Isis was the best known and most revered god for urban social and intellectual elites, and Julia Mamaea was devoted to her, among many other deities.

The emperor's mother heard that Origen knew the writings of the Greek philosophers as well as anyone, but that he was also devoted to Jesus, a deity from Palestine. So when Origen finally arrived at the royal palace, she asked him what aspect of the divine essence Jesus represented.

"None and all," the handsome young North African replied cryptically.

"By Jupiter, what do you mean, young man?"

"If I may be so impertinent, Imperial Mother, I wouldn't call on Jupiter if I were you. But when I say None and All, I mean that Jesus is the fullness of the divine in himself. Therefore there is no one aspect by itself that He represents, because He represents them all."

"Well, I've never heard of such a thing—that the countless aspects of the Divine could all be found in one deity alone. That seems impossible. By the way, why do you say I shouldn't call on Jupiter? He's the king of the gods, and the patron of my son's Empire!"

"Again, Imperial Mother, don't dismiss me as superstitious or irreligious when I say what I am about to say. But you know full well that the cosmos is full of spirits and divinities. You also know that not all these spirits are benign."

"Yes, of course! We all know these things. I am not an ignoramus."

"Of course not. You are well known for your life of piety, and your broad-mindedness."

"You flatter me."

"No, I am speaking the truth. And here's another truth, taught by the

---

[3]A Greco-Roman school of philosophy, dating from the late fourth century B.C.E., that believed God to be the immanent all-pervading energy by which the natural world is created and sustained. This divine energy communicates its moral law through the order and beauty of the world. The Stoics called this energy *logos* (reason or word). The apostle John then said Jesus is the Logos (Jn 1:1).

God of the Cosmos, apart from whom there is no other: there are de-mons behind the names of many so-called gods."

"Demons? Behind Jupiter? How can you utter such blasphemy?"

"Please be patient, Imperial Mother. If Jupiter really is the name of the highest god, or just another name for the Divinity of divinity, then utter-ing his name would be no different from uttering the name of other gods such as Amon, the Egyptian god, or Pappaeus, whom the Scythians call the 'Supreme God.'"

Origen paused, to make sure Julia was still listening. She was. "But it does make a difference. When people merely aspirate these sounds, call-ing upon these names to manifest themselves, suddenly real spiritual pow-ers come. Yet they aren't like the peaceful and good creator of all things. They are often petty and angry, contemptuous of us human beings.

"This is why the ancient Jewish prophets said the gods were demons. At one time God the Creator allotted the nations to them. Perhaps at that time they were angels. But then they wanted to be worshiped as the first and highest God, and they gradually turned malevolent, leading their peoples away from the worship of the true God."[4]

The emperor's mother was puzzled. "Then who is Jesus? What does he have to do with the true god?"

"He is the only Son of the true God. He came to Palestine in the flesh, healing and doing good, and rising from the dead to prove His divine credentials."

"Can I join his sacred mysteries, just as I did for Isis and Osiris?"

"These mysteries are very different. Jesus requires you to repent of all your sins, and to allow Him to bring complete moral and spiritual trans-formation to your life."

Julia Mamaea went on for several days, picking Origen's brain, trying to find out how Jesus was different from the other gods, and where his philosophy diverged from the Greek philosophers whom Origen knew so well. He told Julia that while Greek and Christian philosophers shared some ideas, the Christian versions of those ideas were more powerful. Greek ideas could change minds, and only to a point, but Christian faith

---

[4]The preceding dialogue, the exact words of which I have constructed, is based on Origen's discussion of gods' names in chapter 17 of the *Philokalia* and a portion in book 5 of his po-lemical treatise *Against Celsus*, the late second-century pagan critic of Christianity.

could change the heart. If Plato could convince the mind that something is true, only Jesus Christ can show that it is *real*.

There is a second way in which Greek philosophy (which, as you recall from previous chapters, is really a religious approach to life) is different from Christian faith, Origen told the imperial mother. The god of the philosophers can be reached only by the cultured elite—those who have the education to learn the philosophical way and the money to afford the time required to pursue its difficult path. But the Christian God of grace makes it easy to come to him, if only you are humble. It is impossible by human striving to see God, but by a miracle of grace he shows his face to those who humble themselves.

Third, said Origen, is the question of how to find God. Both Plato and Jesus agree that our goal is the vision of God and that we attain that goal by a gradual ascent, through the heavens and supercelestial regions, and eventually to a blissful contemplation of divine things. But they disagree on means. Hellenistic religion uses many gods and rigorous human effort, while Jesus insists there is only one God and his grace alone that lifts us up to himself.[5]

As far as we know, Julia Mamaea never became a Christian. She thought Jesus was just another Hellenistic deity representing one more aspect of divinity. She was not prepared for Origen's insistence that he is the only God, full of all the divine aspects. Nor was she ready to repent of her sins and undergo the moral transformation that Origen insisted was the narrow gate for those wanting to convert.

"The Greatest Teacher After the Apostles"

This young evangelist/theologian went on to become one of the Christian church's greatest theologians. The fourth-century biblical scholar Jerome said Origen was the greatest teacher of the church after the apostles.[6] His *De principiis (On First Principles)* was the first systematic theology, the first Christian attempt at a coherent interpretation of Christianity as a whole. Over the course of his career, Origen wrote somewhere between one and two thousand works, most of which were tragically

---

[5]These arguments against Greek philosophy can be found in Origen's *Against Celsus*.
[6]Later in his life, when Origen's work came under suspicion of heresy, Jerome changed his mind.

destroyed by the same man (Emperor Justinian) who built Hagia Sophia, the greatest church building of the first millennium. Origen's impact on later Christian thinking was profound, influencing Eusebius and the Cappadocian theologians (Basil the Great, Gregory of Nazianzus and Gregory of Nyssa), Maximus the Confessor, Hilary of Poitiers and Ambrose of Milan. He who "tower[ed] above the Greek fathers as Augustine tower[ed] above the Latins,"[7] has also been called the "ancestor of the great monastic movement of the fourth century."[8]

But Origen was not just a theologian. Above all, he was a teacher of the Bible, with a pastor's heart. The pastoral challenges he faced sound remarkably similar to those facing pastors in the twenty-first century. Immersed in a culture more interested in undemanding pantheism than rigorous discipleship, many Christians gave scant attention to their own religion, were more concerned with pleasure and commerce, and even when in church wanted to be titillated with amusing stories rather than difficult strictures from the Scriptures. Listen to an excerpt from one of Origen's sermons:

> The Lord has entrusted me with the task of giving his household their allowance of food [Bible teaching] at the appointed time [Lk 12:42]. . . . But how can I? Where and when can I find a time when you will listen to me? The greater part of your time, nearly all of it in fact, you spend on mundane things, in the market-place or the shops; some of you are busy in the country, others wrapped up in litigation. Nobody, or hardly anybody, bothers about God's Word. . . . But why complain about those who are not here? Even those who are, those of you who have come to church, are paying no attention. You can take an interest in tales that have become worn out through repetition, but you turn your backs on God's Word and the reading of Holy Scripture.[9]

Origen complained that some stood in the corner of church and gabbed while the Bible was being read or preached. He lamented that although he urged the young men to study the Bible, he had wasted his time. "None" seemed to take his suggestion.

---

[7]G. W. Butterworth, introduction to Origen, *On First Principles,* with an introduction to the Torchbook ed. by Henri De Lubac (Gloucester, Mass.: Peter Smith, 1973), p. xxvii.
[8]Jean Danielou, *Origen,* trans. Walter Mitchell (New York: Sheed & Ward, 1955), p. vii.
[9]*Homilies on Genesis* 10.1; cited in Danielou, *Origen,* p. 42.

An Extraordinary Life

Before we study Origen's remarkable reflections on other religions, let's take a brief look at his life. Born in 185 to Christian parents, probably in Alexandria, Origen was something of a child prodigy. Encouraged by his father, the boy not only memorized huge portions of the Bible but eagerly probed their deeper meaning. His father, delighted by his son's love for the Lord and the Bible, would go to the sleeping boy at night and kiss his breast "as if it was the temple of a divine spirit," blessing God for being given such a promising child.[10]

When Septimius Severus launched a persecution of the church in 202, seventeen-year-old Origen begged his father not to waver: "Mind you, don't change your mind on our account."[11] His father apparently listened to his son, for he perished in the attacks. Origen himself was prevented from fulfilling his desire for martyrdom only when his mother hid his clothes.

Because of his prodigious ability and the loss of teachers to persecution, Origen was made head of the church's catechetical school within a year of his father's death. By night he studied the Bible and by day he prepared his students for martyrdom.

> For not only when they were in prison, or were being cross-examined, up to the final sentence, but even when they were afterwards led away to execution, he was at the side of the holy martyrs, displaying astonishing fearlessness and meeting danger face to face. As he boldly approached and fearlessly greeted the martyrs with a kiss, again and again the maddened crowd of pagans that surrounded him were on the point of stoning him.[12]

Moving from house to house to avoid those plotting against him, Origen fasted from both food and sleep in his effort to grow closer to God. For several years he went without shoes, abstained from wine and subsisted on a minimum of nourishment. After a time he started a school similar to Justin Martyr's in Rome, teaching Greek philosophy to all who cared to hear. Thousands flocked to hear him. Those familiar with philosophy

---

[10]Eusebius *History of the Church* 6.2.
[11]Eusebius *History of the Church* 6.2.
[12]Eusebius *History of the Church* 6.3.

remarked that his knowledge of the classics was unparalleled.

When Origen was nearly thirty, he was asked by two bishops in Palestine to move there to preach and teach. While there, the bishop of Alexandria excommunicated Origen, probably because he was jealous of Origen's renown.

In 249, when Decius unleashed his cruel persecution of Christians, Origen was granted his wish to suffer for Christ. Eusebius writes of the sixty-five-year-old's "agony in iron and the darkness of his prison; how for days on end his legs were pulled four paces apart in the torturer's stocks—the courage with which he bore threats of fire and every torture devised by his enemies," and of the "messages full of help for those in need of comfort."[13] Origen was released from prison before he died, but his health was broken. Death came shortly after.

Bad Reputation

Despite his holiness, devotion and theological influence, Origen's reputation has suffered under a cloud to this day. There are two reasons. First, in a fit of teenage religious zeal, he castrated himself. Eusebius explains that this was an attempt, in an uncharacteristically literalist reading, to fulfill his Savior's observation that some "made themselves eunuchs for the sake of the kingdom of heaven" (Mt 19:12).[14] The other reason is a number of his teachings that were later judged to be heretical. The most notorious was his suggestion that all creatures might eventually be saved, including the devil himself. There is also dispute about whether he suggested the possibility of the transmigration of souls (reincarnation).

Origen, however, never advanced these, or any other irregular ideas, as dogmatic doctrines. As many historians have observed, he "put forward his views for discussion, not as settled dogmas."[15] Origen feared heresy, arguing it would destroy the church. Eusebius tells us Origen kept "from his earliest years the rule of the Church and 'abominat[ed]'— the very word he uses somewhere himself—all heretical teachings."[16] He

---

[13]Eusebius *History of the Church* 6.39.
[14]Eusebius *History of the Church* 6.8.
[15]Butterworth, introduction to *On First Principles*, p. xxxvii.
[16]Eusebius *History of the Church* 6.2.

advanced new ideas only tentatively, always acknowledging the church's right to condemn them if they were contrary to the rule of faith. Some of his ideas were later condemned as heretical, but he was never formally a heretic because his erroneous opinions were always concerning questions which at that time had not been settled. He was bound, he said, to church teaching. "But[, for instance,] what existed before this world, or what will exist after it, has not yet been made known openly to the many, for no clear statement on the point is set forth in the Church teaching."[17]

His questionable teachings were usually developed in attempts to undermine other heresies. For example, Origen emphasized human freedom in order to combat the Gnostics who said there is nothing you can do to change your eternal fate. Origen imagined that freedom must be an eternal constant—hence the freedom of even the devils and the damned to change their minds. Long after Origen's death, the church condemned this idea. But should we discount everything else this teacher of the church wrote because he tentatively explored questions that the church had not yet settled?

Origen declared himself to be a *vir ecclesiasticus* (man of the church), and insisted that he would never knowingly violate any church doctrine. In fact, if the church decided that any part of his teaching was in error, he hoped the church would condemn it.

> I bear the title of priest and, as you see, I preach the Word of God. But if I do anything contrary to the discipline of the Church or the rule laid down in the Gospels—if I give offence to you and to the Church—then I hope the whole Church will unite with one consent and cast me off.[18]

Words to the Wise

Now we are in a position to look at Origen's teachings on non-Christian religions. Surprisingly, we find that he who is often dismissed as a heretic warns Christians to be careful with other religions, lest they unwittingly be led into heresy. His first warning is that only mature Christians should investigate other religions. For them, the wisdom of other reli-

---

[17]*On First Principles,* preface 7.
[18]*Homily on Joshua* 7.6; cited in Danielou, *Origen,* p. 8.

gious teachers can be profitable. But what is profitable to the mature can be fatal to baby or immature Christians. Only those who "have received full knowledge of the truth" should wade into the murky waters of non-Christian theology. Teachers and pastors, he said, must always be on the alert "not to wound those who still have little training in Christ" by introducing them to teachings that are too advanced for them to understand properly. This was why the apostle Paul said there is a "secret and hidden" wisdom that he shared only with the "mature" (1 Cor 2:6-7).

But even the mature need to be wary, said Origen. The philosophy of this world is dangerous because, along with its truth, there is serious error. (Once more we see that when thinkers in this age wrote of "philosophy," they meant rational systems that were the equivalent of what we call "religions" today: declarations about the nature of reality and rules for how to live. They were religious as much as philosophical—just as Hindu and Buddhist religions include philosophical analyses of reality as well as advice on how to live. Therefore I will use the phrase "other religions" for systems of thought that Origen called "philosophies.") Because other religions can lead a person away from the true God, no compromise with their philosophies is possible. Their attractions are like the food dedicated to idols, which Paul warned against in his first letter to the church at Corinth. Origen also referred to Achan, the young man whose theft caused the Israelites to be defeated at Ai in Joshua 7; other religions are similar to the bar of gold that Achan stole—a cursed object that seduces with its shining beauty but contaminates a whole people. Alien philosophies and religions invariably leave those who follow them with uncertainty and doubt.

That doesn't mean other religions have no use at all. Their principal use for the Christian is to help unbelievers come to faith. They help lay a kind of intellectual foundation by preparing people for the higher and deeper truths of Christ. This is what we have already seen in some other Fathers—the religions as *praeparatio evangelica* (preparation for the gospel). In a letter to his former pupil, St. Gregory the Wonderworker, Origen said that his students could advance the Christian cause by making full use of what Greek thought had achieved.

> I am therefore very desirous that you should accept such parts even of
> Greek philosophy as may serve for the ordinary elementary instruction of

our schools, and be a kind of *preparation for Christianity:* also those portions of geometry and astronomy likely to be of use in the interpretation of the sacred Scriptures, so that, what the pupils of the philosophers say about geometry and music, grammar, rhetoric, and astronomy, viz. that they are the handmaidens of philosophy, we may say of philosophy itself in relation to Christianity.[19]

Origen told Gregory that the Bible suggests this use of other religions when the children of Israel, on their way out of Egypt, are "told to ask their neighbors and companions for vessels of silver and gold, and for clothing, so that by 'spoiling the Egyptians' they might find materials to make the things of which they were told for the divine service." Out of these spoils came the contents of the Holy of Holies, the ark with its cover, and the Cherubim, mercy seat, and golden pot in which were hidden the manna. All of these, "we may suppose," were made from this Egyptian gold. From the second-best gold probably came the candlestick and lamps, the golden table and the gold censer. The clothing was most likely rewoven to make the veils and curtains for the sanctuary in the wilderness.[20]

Therefore pagan learning and religion can be good for teaching the gospel to others. But it is not good for actually learning things about God. Pagan philosophy and thinking on subjects such as geometry and astronomy can help us understand the Bible. But only the Bible can tell us who the true God is and what he is like.

So we should sift the good from the bad when we approach other religions. Gregory said that "in every philosophy [Origen] picked out what was true and useful and set it before us, while what was erroneous was rejected."[21]

If some Christians objected that we should never learn from pagan religion and philosophy, Origen retorted that the patriarchs were willing to enter into unions with concubines or alien women, even in old age, so that they could bring forth children in chastity. If we can convert a few to the faith, such use of pagan thinking is justified. When we use

---

[19] *Philokalia* 13.1; emphasis added.
[20] *Philokalia* 13.1.
[21] Gregory, "Oration and Panegyric Addressed to Origen" XIV, in *Ante-Nicene Fathers*, vol. 6 (Grand Rapids: Eerdmans, 1978), p. 36.

pagan methods more faithfully to the truth than pagans themselves, and get other pagans to accept the true philosophy of Christ, "then we can say that we have had children by dialectic or rhetoric, as by an alien woman or concubine."[22]

Moses did the same thing, Origen said. He accepted the counsel of his father-in-law, Jethro the pagan priest. Therefore, "if we happen to find a word of wisdom on the lips of a pagan, we should not immediately disdain the word itself because of the speaker; because it is not right to swell with pride and scorn the words of wise men on the pretext that we possess a law given to us by God. Rather, as the Apostle says, we must test everything and retain what is good."[23] While all truth comes from above, and there is much truth in other religions, every other religion has been corrupted, to some extent, by the malice of men or demons.

Ironically, then, it is from one who is often regarded as a heretic that we are warned to be careful about speculations coming from Justin, Irenaeus and Clement—three Fathers the church has always included within orthodoxy. Origen did not share their optimism about the religions and philosophies of the Greco-Roman world. Perhaps that is because he, unlike these three Fathers, had grown up as a Christian. In fact, Origen wrote at some length about people of faith who had been led astray by other religions and philosophies.

> The Divine Scripture knows, however, that some were the worse for the going down of the children of Israel from their own land into Egypt, and darkly hints that some do lose by sojourning with the Egyptians, that is to say, by lingering in the learning of the world after being nourished in the law of God and the Divine worship of Israel.[24]

Hadad the Edomite, Origen pointed out, did fine as long as he remained in the land of Israel. But once he "ran away from wise Solomon" and went down to Egypt, his faith began to be corrupted (1 Kings 11:14-22). He married Pharaoh's wife's sister, and they bore a son who was raised among Pharaoh's sons. All this meant that he had "run away from the wisdom of God." It was no wonder that when he returned to Israel, he

---

[22]Origen, location of quotation unspecified, in Henri de Lubac, introduction to *On First Principles*, p. xvi.
[23]Ibid.
[24]*Philokalia* 13.3.

turned Israel to the worship of a golden calf.

Origen warned that this is all too often what happens to Christians who dabble in other religions: "A man is seldom found who takes the useful things of Egypt, leaves that land, and provides for the service of God." The problem is that "Hadad the Edomite has many a brother." These are the ones who become infatuated with other religions, are able to skillfully use their new knowledge, mix that knowledge illegitimately with Scripture, and then import new and foreign meanings into Scripture. Just as Hadad told Israel that it was really the golden calf that had delivered her from Egypt.[25]

The Hellenistic Dilemma

Origen thought long and hard about the central question of this book—why are there other religions at all? If the Christian faith is the fullest revelation of God to human beings, why did this all-powerful God permit the rise and flourishing of other creeds and traditions?

Origen did not ask the question in precisely this way. Instead, he and his age asked why there was such diversity of rank in the cosmos. Nearly everyone believed that the heavens (there were plenty of them), both lower and higher, were full of angels and powers (the sorts we have discussed in the previous chapters) and spirits, both good and bad. The sixty-four-thousand dollar question then was why the cosmos had turned out this way, with radically different degrees of happiness for those on different ranks—angelic, spiritual and human. It was not such a compelling dilemma for the majority who were either polytheists or pantheists. For them, there was no one god in control of all and who claimed to be good. Things were as they were simply because they were. Some called this Fate.

But for Jews and Christians, this was a problem. Their God, they said, was good and all-powerful. So how was all the diversity to be explained? Especially when the diversity seemed to be unjust—when good people were on the bottom of the human ranks, and manifestly evil people were at the top?

Today we call this the problem of evil. People in the Hellenistic age

---

[25]*Philokalia* 13.3.

did not put it quite in these terms, perhaps because, contrary to most moderns, they were not convinced that human nature is good. Hence many evils befalling us humans could be written off to the consequences/punishment for sin. Their question was different: Why is the cosmos structured with so many, many levels and ranks? Why were people and spirits born on different grades of the cosmic chain of being? How can the infinite variations in the cosmos be just? And why do different races have different advantages in civilization and religion?

Origen was acutely aware of this problem, and the entire structure of his theology can be seen as his answer to the question. As we see how his theology works, it will become clear how he tried to resolve this Hellenistic dilemma. In the process, it will also become clear that he thought he knew why there are other religions.

History, the Fall and Preexistence

For Origen, it all goes back to the Fall. Not only the human Fall in Eden, but also and especially the angelic Fall in the heavens. In the divine primordium, before the creation, the heavens were full of created spirits, and every one of these spirits was absolutely equal. Thus—and here is Origen's fundamental theological move that controlled the rest of his theology—all diversity that now exists in cosmic history is a result of merits and demerits.

Spirits either obeyed or disobeyed God, and in varying degrees of each. This infinite variation in response to God gave rise to the infinitely diverse hierarchies of angels and people, races and conditions of humans, and even the heavenly bodies. The latter are living beings with souls, who are capable of responding to God.[26]

The biggest sinners became demons. Those who sinned less became angels; those who sinned least were made archangels. Still others were not sinful enough to become demons, but were too sinful to become angels. So they were given bodies and became human beings. All of this was strictly just, in keeping with their sins. God showed that he was not a respecter of persons.

---

[26] *On First Principles* 1.7.3.

Freedom and Justice

All diversity, then, is a result of God's gift of freedom to his rational, spiritual creatures. "The position of every created being is the result of his own work and his known motives." That means that all the power that is now exerted by heavenly beings and by powerful humans "is not by some privilege of creation but as the reward of merit."[27] In all ages and worlds, invisible and visible, all beings "are arranged in a definite order proportionate to the degree and excellence of their merits."[28]

The angels, then, are angels and not humans or demons because they were rewarded for their zeal and virtue, displayed before the creation. It was not by chance or random events, but by merit, that one angel was given the church at Ephesus and another the church at Smyrna (Rev 2). Otherwise, Origen argued, God would be partial, which would mean unjust.

This also explains human diversity. Some babies are born blind because of sins they committed in preexistence. Some are born in good climates, conducive to trade and civilization, while others are born in regions far from the comforts of developed culture. Once again, freedom and the merits and demerits that follow in its train explain it all.

And most importantly for our purposes, freedom and merit partly explain religious diversity. Jacob was preferred by God because "in some previous life" he had done things worthy of merit. This is why Israel was God's chosen people—of all the nations, she was the only one to remain true to God. It also explains why some nations got more revelation than others. The Word appeared to human beings only to the extent they deserved it. That in turn was a function of how much they resembled the Word morally and spiritually. As they made choices to respond to what little revelation they had, God gave them more. If they turned away from revelation in nature and conscience, God took away what little they had by hardening their hearts. This holds true for salvation: God fills with the Holy Spirit and sanctifies only those who deserve it.[29]

Origen argued that we choose for God only when we accept spiritual progress. If we stop at any stage and become self-satisfied, we are mov-

---

[27] *On First Principles* 1.5.3.
[28] *On First Principles* 1.6.3.
[29] *On First Principles* 1.7.4.

ing down and away from God. This principle is at work not just in individuals but also in whole religions. The Jews, for example, refused to leave their past behind and move on to the next stage of recognizing that Jesus is the Messiah.

But it is never too late. Further rise is always possible, because God loves us enough to keep us free. Some men became so good by free choice that they were taken up to become angels. These are what the Bible calls "sons of God" or "sons of the resurrection." Some became so perfect that they became "of one spirit with Him" (1 Cor 6:17).

It is also possible to fall. This is darkly hinted in Ezekiel 28, where the prince of Tyre is cast down from heaven. This must refer to "some angel, to whom had been allotted the duty of supervising the Tyrian people, whose souls also were apparently committed to his care." And when Isaiah 14 speaks of Lucifer "fallen from heaven" because he wanted to ascend into heaven and become like the Most High, it means this prince of darkness was once a light-bearer. He was once good. But then he became an apostate.

This also means that no one is stainless by nature (even a great angel can fall), and no one is polluted essentially (all were created good, and still have enough goodness in them to be free). But we must be wary. For these examples show us, says Origen, that sloth and negligence may cause us to "progress" to such an extent that we are changed into "opposing powers." We humans can become not only demonic but evil powers in league with the prince of darkness.[30]

Providence and Evil

If freedom is the first controlling principle for Origen's theology, providence is the other. By the latter I mean God's overall supervision of everything that happens in the cosmos. Nothing takes place that is outside of his control and permission. As Origen liked to quote, Jesus said that not a sparrow falls to the ground "apart from your Father" (Mt 10:29). This includes free human choices. They are free, but God is also in control. Origen insisted on a rationally understood connection between human diversity and human choices, but he was not so insistent

---

[30] *On First Principles* 1.5.5.

on a rational connection between God's providence and human choices.

How God could control choices that are free without destroying freedom has been a conundrum for millennia for religious thinkers. Origen appealed to the long stretch of history in which God uses the sum total of choices to lead his creatures to himself. God somehow permits and oversees our free choices so as to induce us to return to him of our own free will. "The universe is as it were an immense, monstrous animal, held together by the power and reason of God as by one soul."[31]

This sometimes requires God to act within the human heart—which would seem to overrule any sort of absolute freedom. Or it means that he permits bad choices to continue, thus hardening the sinner's heart. God permits this to some, however, because he knows they will wake up only after they have sunk to the bottom and tasted filth. In a change of metaphor, Origen suggested the abscess must be allowed to burst. In this way, sin is sometimes a step toward salvation—but only because of God's providential supervision of the whole journey. He uses the remedy appropriate to the disease.

God even uses evil for his purposes. Origen was insistent that God does not cause evil. No evil things happen by God's doing. But neither do they happen without God. We cannot doubt this when our Lord tells us that even the sparrow's fall cannot take place without his Father.[32] Job's troubles would not have come to him from the devil unless God permitted it. "In all these circumstances every believer must say, 'Thou wouldst have no power against me, except it were given thee from above.'"[33]

Even when evil appears to be unchecked by God, he is working in hidden ways to purge hearts. God deals with evil hearts in his own mysterious time and ways. "God, while preserving each individual's free will, makes use of the evil of wicked men in the administration of the world, so disposing them as to conduce to the benefit of the whole; nevertheless, such men are deserving of blame."[34]

God, who knows the secrets of the heart and foreknows the future, per-

---

[31] *On First Principles* 2.1.3.
[32] *On First Principles* 3.2.7.
[33] *On First Principles* 3.2.6.
[34] *Against Celsus* 4.70.

haps in his longsuffering allows the hidden evil to remain while he draws it out by means of external circumstances, with the object of purifying him who owing to carelessness has received into himself the seeds of sin, that having vomited them out when they come to the surface the sinner, even though he has proceeded far in evil deeds, may in the end be able to obtain purification after his evil life and be renewed.[35]

God's ways are different, says Origen, because his timeline is far longer than ours: "God deals with souls not in view of the fifty years, so to speak, of our life here, but in view of the endless world." He knows not only the times but also the appropriate means to reach his ends. He "knows how by means of the great plagues and the drowning in the sea he is leading even Pharaoh."[36]

For Origen, then, God is leading every soul to eventual salvation, by means unknown to mortal minds. His creatures' choices are free, but he superintends the process in such a way as to suggest that over the long haul God controls the end result. If the choices of those who hate God are so directed that at last they choose God, we have the impression that choices are not so free and God is more sovereign than first appeared. Most Christians have condemned Origen's teaching of *apocatastasis* (restoration of all things) and what seems to be his works-righteousness (the idea that our human efforts save us). But his long view of history and God's ultimate control shows that for Origen God's freedom finally overwhelms creaturely freedom. In the end, it is not what we want, but what he has gotten us to want.

Spirits, Angels and Demons

When Origen takes up the supernatural world, we see how these twin poles of freedom and providence show us his view of the religions. Origen's view of the cosmos was much like that of his Hellenistic peers—the air and the skies and heavens are bustling with activity and beings. At the top of the hierarchy are angels of various grades; some control what happens down here close to earth at the "sublunary" levels, while others are higher and manage the nations. Then, closer to earth and in

---

[35] *On First Principles* 3.1.13.
[36] *On First Principles* 3.1.14.

our midst are innumerable spirits, both good and bad, that help us and hurt us, depending on their own allegiances and orientations.

Let's start with the angels, for they have the most to do with other religions. Generally, angels are "better" souls who postpone their own bliss in order to help inferior human souls make their way along the spiritual journey to eventually lose their bodies again and become like angels. The lower angels control all the sublunary elements such as fire and water. They are used by the Logos (the Second Person of the Trinity, who has been delegated by the Father to administer the cosmos) to control the movements of the stars and other celestial beings in the heavens, animals and even plants. The higher angels were appointed by God, according to our now-familiar Deuteronomy 32:8 (Origen followed the Septuagint, which translates the Hebrew "sons of God" as "angels of God"), to preside over the nations.

This cosmology was very common in the Hellenistic world, and in fact suited the Roman Empire just fine. For it seemed to validate the empire's own administration by sketching on the spiritual plane what Rome had established politically: local leaders controlled by the overall imperium.

But Origen went further than Roman politicos would find comfortable. For Origen said the cosmos was at war, and there were local battles everywhere. Every nation had both a good angel and a bad angel, and every individual good spirits and bad spirits warring for his soul. The *Pax Romana* did not extend to the spiritual plane; if anything, Origen's map of the spiritual cosmos mirrored the wars and infighting that were beginning to tear apart the empire in its waning centuries.

Origen developed the angelic picture that we saw both in the Bible and the earlier Greek Fathers: the angels were neutral or benevolent when they were first given the nations to administer. And some were still good, such as the angel of Macedonia who requested Paul to come preach there (Acts 16:9). Until Christ came, they struggled to check the idolatry their peoples kept embracing, and so their success was very limited. That's why these angels welcomed Christ's coming at the incarnation and cheered on Paul and the other apostles' preaching around the empire. That's also why some nations and cities received the gospel readily.

But most angels didn't, and this too explains why many nations and cities were resistant to the gospel. These angels had encouraged their nations to worship them instead of God. When they saw that the Lord and Savior was coming to destroy all the doctrines of "what is falsely called knowledge" (1 Tim 6:20), they laid snares for him, not knowing who he really was. But Jesus' identity as the Son of God was revealed when, after they "crucified the Lord of glory," he rose from the dead. That's why Paul said the wisdom we speak "is not a wisdom of this age or of the rulers [*archontes;* ruling powers] of this age, who are doomed to perish. . . . None of the *archontes* of this age understood this; for if they had, they would not have crucified the Lord of glory" (1 Cor 2:6-8).

Yet Origen believed that a few of these *archontes* converted when Christ came. Their conversion, and the conversion of their nations, shows that even evil powers can change sides in the future. It is the majority of angels, Origen believed, who still controlled the nations of his day and were responsible therefore not only for their resistance to the gospel, but also for the religions to which their peoples were devoted. These were, among others, "the secret and hidden philosophy of the Egyptians and the astrology of the Chaldeans and Indians, who profess a knowledge of high things, and further the manifold and diverse opinion of the Greeks concerning the divine nature."[37]

Both Origen's parishioners and the seekers who were drawn to Origen's spellbinding teaching wondered (a) if there was truth in these other religions that were controlled by "bad" angels and (b) if the angels taught these mixed or false doctrines sincerely or maliciously. We've already seen Origen's answer to the first question: most of the religions are mixtures of truth and falsehood. Hence Christians must approach them warily and sift truth from error. Origen's answer to the second question is perhaps more interesting.

First let us hear the way Origen put the question:

> The question indeed arises whether these varieties of wisdom which belong to the rulers of this world and with which they strive to indoctrinate men are introduced into our minds by the opposing powers with the desire of ensnaring and injuring us, or whether they are offered to us simply in consequence of an error, that is, not with a view to injuring men but because the "rulers of this world" themselves think their wisdom to be true

---

[37] *On First Principles* 3.3.2.

and are therefore anxious to teach others what in their opinion is the truth.[38]

Origen's answer is that the latter is "more likely" the case. They are probably like "Greek authors or leaders of various heresies," who originally accepted a false doctrine in place of the truth because they sincerely believed the former, and have tried to persuade others of what they think, erroneously, to be true.

While that may be true for some of the "opposing powers," it is not true for all. Those who get their falsehoods taught in the churches, who "teach another doctrine of Christ than that which the rule of scripture allows," are those "apostate and exiled powers" that teach their heresies "either from the pure wickedness of their mind and will or else from envy." They are jealous of the powers that have "seen the light" and converted, and who now are on the way of ascent toward the light.[39] They want to prevent these powers and their human subjects from making progress toward the Truth. Even, and especially, in the spiritual world, misery loves company.

After the angels are other spirits, more benign in influence, that are responsible for human culture. They are what Origen calls "certain special energies of this world" that have chosen, by their own free will, to inspire "poetry, geometry, and the originator of each art and subject of instruction." The Greeks, Origen remarks, know of these spirits of culture. They know that "the art of poetry cannot exist apart from madness." Seers are said by their historians to be suddenly filled with a "certain kind of madness" (Origen might have been thinking of Plato's *Phaedrus* 245 A). Then there are those who are called "divine" because by the power of "daemons" (not evil but cultural) that possess them for a time, they spontaneously compose verses according to complex "rules of the poetic art." This has happened to boys "of tender age." The priestess of the Delphic oracle is another example of this. We can understand it, Origen explains, by thinking of saints who are of such "holy and stainless souls" that they acquire thereby a communion with the divine nature and are given prophecy and other spiritual gifts. In a similar way, those

---

[38] *On First Principles* 3.3.3.
[39] *On First Principles* 3.3.4.

who show themselves "fit subjects for the opposing powers" become inspired by these powers and participate "in their wisdom and doctrine." The result is that they are filled with the spirits which they serve.[40]

Finally, at the more pedestrian level, are ordinary folks like us. We too, says Origen, are beset by both good and bad spirits. There are guardian devils that try to keep Gentiles in the national cults, controlled by the bad angels, and there are guardian angels also seeking to win souls to the truth. The letter to the Hebrews speaks of "ministering spirits" sent out to serve those who are to inherit salvation (Heb 1:14 NASB). The apostles and prophets were clearly influenced by these good spirits.

Bad spirits, or demons, first gain entrance to the soul through "intemperance." If the individual does not fight back by striving for virtue, these bad spirits take possession. The possession may be total and long-lasting, or the demons may just deprave the soul through harmful suggestions. This is what happened to Judas, who was incited to betrayal by the devil's placing that thought strongly in his consciousness. Judas was still responsible for listening to and then obeying this thought, but there was strong external influence as well.[41]

At this point Origen used his theory of preexistence to explain why some are controlled by bad spirits and others by good. It goes back to sins committed before birth. This is why, he suggests, John the Baptist was already leaping with the Holy Spirit in the womb, and Jeremiah was known by God as a fetus. It also helps us know why some people seem to be possessed by a demon from their earliest years, or, say, by a spirit of ventriloquism (such as the slave girl in Acts 16:16). Some are born in suffering because divine providence judged them guilty of a previous sin and therefore worthy of punishment.[42]

While we modern Christians are astonished that a Christian, particularly a learned Christian such as Origen, could believe something that seems so unbiblical (we think of Jesus refuting this very theory when the disciples asked him about the man born blind in John 9:1-3), we must remember that this probably did not trigger much astonishment in Origen's day. Preexistence of the soul came from Platonism, which was the

---

[40]Ibid. 3.3.3; on the Delphic oracle, see Origen *Against Celsus* 3.25 and 7.3.
[41]*On First Principles* 3.3.4-5.
[42]*On First Principles* 3.3.5.

dominant philosophy of the time. To some Christians as well as other Hellenists, this seemed to be an elegant and commonsense explanation of suffering and evil. We should also recall that Origen advanced this theory tentatively, and never made it required doctrine for his pupils.

Reasons for Religious Diversity

Let's gather together now Origen's explanation of religious diversity. As Origen himself put it, the reason why most people have different religions is because they were born among peoples for whom one religion was dominant and they know very little of anything else. That's the human side of the answer. From the divine side, it goes back to the Fall and the history of salvation ever since. God apportioned the nations to different angels on the basis of, first, their responses to God before they took bodies, and later, on the basis of the spiritual capacities of their peoples—which in turn were results of what they did as premortal spirits.

There is no chance, then, in the variations of religions among humanity. It is not an accident that someone is born into a family of Ethiopians, whose religion tells them to feed on human flesh. Nor is it by chance that a soul is born among the Scythians, where their religion permits them to kill their fathers. Or that someone is raised as a Taurian, whose religion tells them to offer strangers up in sacrifice.[43] Even the worship of the stars and planets, which to the Christian seems evil, has a reason. This form of idolatry was actually permitted by God as the lesser of several evils. God permitted it to peoples whom he knew were incapable (at the time) of knowing the true God, who is pure spirit. But this worship of benign (but living!) material powers protected these peoples from the worship of truly demonic powers, which were far worse.[44]

Can we learn anything from all this? I think we can. If we put aside our natural (and largely correct!) prejudices against his wild speculations about preexistence and reincarnation and the possibility of salvation even for the devil, there are several important principles that can help us answer some of the questions with which this book started.

---

[43] *On First Principles* 2.9.5.

[44] Henri de Lubac, introduction to the Torchbook ed. of Origen, *On First Principles* (Gloucester, Mass.: Peter Smith, 1973), pp. 113-14.

We can learn from his warnings that exploration of other religions is deep water that the spiritually young should not enter until they have first gone deeper into their own pools. Even mature Christians should know that there are riptides and other currents that could carry them out to sea. Some have never returned to land.

Not that there isn't truth and other helpful things in the religions. There are. Origen himself pointed to wonderful truths that Christians can use to help lead seekers to the fuller religious Truth. They can also help public apologists set forth the intellectual coherence of Christian faith in the public arena—by showing the ways in which questions raised by the religions are answered by Christ, or even perhaps the explicit pointers in the religions to things taught but only implicitly in the Scriptures.

Origen also, and more importantly for our task in this book, helps show us that other religions exist not simply for geographical and socio-logical reasons, but also and more importantly for spiritual reasons. We may not agree with the particular ways in which Origen details their his-tories. Most of us cannot buy into the elaborate cosmic vision that Ori-gen taught. But we can learn from him that the religions arose from spir-itual causes, and that some of these causes might have been real and living entities.

We may also consider that they are a mixed bag. They may not all have been evil at the beginning, and some of their teachings, which make up the world religions today, may contain truth that goes back to divine sources. And perhaps this is why we cannot disagree with everything other religions teach. Some degree of divine origin may also be why we find real spiritual resonance with some dimensions of the religions.

9

WHAT *ARE* THE RELIGIONS?
AND WHY ARE THEY THERE?

Collecting the Strands

WHAT CAN WE LEARN ABOUT THE WORLD RELIGIONS from the Bible and these early church Fathers? Perhaps the best place to start is to recall the basic points of each chapter.

Scanning the Highlights

In the first two chapters we saw that the God of the Bible wants all nations to know him. In fact, many non-Jews and non-Christians did indeed know a lot about the true God. Sometimes God's people learned truths about God from things given by God to their pagan neighbors.

In chapter three we saw that there are four different views of the religions in the Old Testament: neighborly pluralism (the gods were created by Yahweh and can be honored as long as God's people can worship Yahweh), competitive pluralism (there is no room for honor to or worship of other gods), vehement missionary exclusivism (there is only one God who exists at all) and cosmic warfare (there are supernatural powers animating the religions, and they are at war with Yahweh and his kingdom).

While at first these views may seem to be competing and contradictory, more careful inspection shows otherwise. They really are complementary. If the biblical and early church thinkers were right, "the gods" are the remnants of primeval angelic powers, once created by Yahweh, but who later turned in rebellion against the Creator. Therefore they may be acknowledged as real and formidable creations of God, while at the same time only Yahweh is to be worshiped as the true God. And only he exists as the source and sustainer of all that is. In the meantime, history's conflicts reflect supernatural conflict in invisible realms between Yahweh and parts of the creation still fighting the Creator. This does not mean that everything in the religions is a manifestation of supernatural powers, anymore than everything Christians do is directed by the Holy Spirit. But it does suggest that we should be attentive to the presence of the spiritual dimension when confronting other religions.

In chapter four we learned of Paul's suggestion that while the powers and principalities seek to undermine God's redemptive plans, God co-opts their seditious designs by using their work to support his own purposes. They use God's law to keep people in bondage to legalistic religion, but God uses their distortions to enforce respect for divine law. We also saw that Paul believed some Greek poets spoke truth about God. Therefore we would not be going too far to think that for Paul other religions might know certain truths about God. Thus the origins of at least some religions are supernatural; they teach some limited truths; and God uses them in his work of redemption.

In chapter five we saw that Justin Martyr went a step further. He argued that some parts of some pagan religions—in his case, Greek philosophical religion—are actually inspired by Christ. According to Justin, all poets and philosophers who teach truth are followers of Christ insofar as they follow those truths. But they don't have full knowledge of God because they don't have personal knowledge of Jesus Christ.

Irenaeus, the great father of salvation history (chapter six), taught that God has always been at work in all the religions, working by the Word. Just as God revealed himself and his plan only in stages, as he progressively trained his people through history, so too God might be using the religions in a developmental way to prepare the nations to receive the fullness of the gospel. But that did not mean for Irenaeus that God saves through other religions. Righteous pagans are saved only by responding to gospel preaching—in Hades on Holy Saturday, in history by hearing the apostles and their successors, and in the millennium. One might infer from Irenaean principles that just as God preached the truth of his Son in various ways conditioned by historical circumstances, so too God might be using the religions in ways conditioned by their historical particularities.

Clement of Alexandria (chapter seven) agreed with Irenaeus that God was in charge of all of history and that the religions were part of his plan to sum up all things in Christ. God even gave some religions as "covenants" to the Gentiles, comparable to the covenant of the Law which he gave to the Jews. All these covenants were meant to lead people to Christ, the fulfillment of all the promises in the covenants. Clement boldly stated that some Gentile religious teachers were "prophets" given by God (but fundamentally different from biblical prophets) and that some defective religions were permitted by God in order to keep their devotees from destruction. They were permitted as secondary way stations on the path to fullness of faith in Christ.

Origen (chapter eight) warned that exploration of the religions is dangerous—potentially destructive for young believers. He particularly highlighted the spiritual nature of other religions, cautioning that malevolent spirits were behind Christianity's rivals. While the religions must be learned by Christian teachers, especially those helping seekers find the truth, they were live coals that could do permanent damage if not handled rightly.

Why Did God Permit Other Religions?

Now for the question we have kept addressing throughout this book: If God has shown his fullest truth in Jesus Christ, and he wants all the world to know the truth, why has he permitted the rise and flourishing of the other great religions? We have seen a number of different and complex answers—some direct and others indirect—to this question in the Bible and early Fathers. Let me try to collect these tangled strands and rearrange them into something that looks like a clear line of thinking.

The early Fathers suggest that the answers to this question go back to God's love. That is, God loved the world so much that he gave its inhabitants freedom to reject his truth, both in whole and in part. Most human beings and civilizations have accepted various dimensions of God's truth, but none has accepted them all. Every one, in fact, has rejected the basic proposition that God be Lord over every area of life. That rejection is what the tradition has called original sin.

Yet God, in his love, has not left humankind in its sins. He has gone back to the world in suffering love, in Christ, to win it back, to redeem it. And he has gone back over and over to work with individuals and cultures, to meet them where they are in their blindness and hardness of heart—in various kinds of blindness and hardness that differ from individual to individual and culture to culture—and to patiently lead them back over time, and indeed millennia, to fuller and fuller visions of the Truth, which is Jesus Christ.

In the moral sphere, an example of God's willingness to work with human beings even in their hardness of heart is divorce. Jesus taught that God's original intention is marriage for life, but that Moses permitted divorce "because you were so hard-hearted, . . . but from the beginning it was not so" (Mt 19:8). Notice the pattern: God permits what is less than the best because his creatures refuse to accept the best. Rather than abandon his creatures because of their stubbornness, God works with them where they are. And by a long process of education and discipline, as God did through Jesus in teaching the original vision of marriage, humans are called to a higher truth.

Irenaeus was the first to portray God as the cosmic pedagogue who educates his creatures through various stages. He taught the Jews by stages, over the course of millennia, in order to prepare them for the Messiah and the gospel. To use the principle we have just examined, God patiently endured Jewish hardness of heart over centuries, gradually softening their hearts and opening their minds to prepare them for the visible incarnation of deity.

In a similar way, we could say, because God respects the freedom of his human creatures, he chose to work with them even when they rejected the fullness of truth and accepted various religious distortions that arose since the Fall. God did not abandon Jews and Christians who accepted divorce, but worked alongside that "marital system" (if you will), honoring what was true in it (the notion of marital covenant and faithfulness within each marriage) while patiently teaching his people to see the higher vision of lifelong marital covenant.

According to Clement, God worked in a similar way with other religions. They are covenants of sorts, comparable to the covenant God gave to the Jews. Within the covenantal system, portions of which, like divorce, are not God's highest will, God gently and gradually led his people toward the new covenant with Jesus.

Of course the Fathers emphasized that there is still a qualitative difference between other religious covenants and the one with the Jews. The former are usually inspired by fallen angels and therefore full of distortions and untruth, while the latter is inspired by the Spirit and full of shadows and images that point to Christ. Real and direct knowledge of the triune God was possible through the Jewish covenant, but only indirect and partial contact with the Logos was possible through the Gentile covenants, which contained inspiration from the Logos only here and there.

Yet the Fathers believed the Gentile covenants (read "religions") saved many from utter destruction. By this they meant that many had no access to the full truth because of the prejudices of their cultures. But the religions of their cultures contained a mixture of truth and error, and the truth saved them from atheism, materialism or spiritual independence. There was enough truth from God in these religions to enable people to respond to God with gratitude and reverence (see Rom 1:21), appreciation for his law written on their hearts (Rom 2:14-15) and recognition that they need grace to cover their sins. This would help prepare them to respond favorably to the gospel—on Holy Saturday or in a postmortem encounter or in the millennium.

Therefore God permitted these religions because of his grace and forbearance toward human hardness of heart. He used what was true within the religions—and these truths were scattered by the Logos—to help prepare whole cultures (not to mention individuals) for eventually receiving the gospel. Even the truth that is distorted within the religions—such as pervasive legalism—is used by God to teach respect for his law, which is fortuitous preparation for seeing Christ as the fulfillment of the Law and for realizing that law cannot give them the perfection they need to live in God's presence.

The early church Fathers believed there were other purposes as well for the religions. First, as Clement put it, was the didactic (for the purpose of teaching). Knowledge of the religions can help teachers of the gospel show seekers how Christ answers questions posed by the human condition and the best of the culture's interrogators. Second, the religions are good for apologetics. God can show the church through the religions how Christ is the fulfillment of all the religious yearnings expressed by other cultures.

And third, the religions are good for theology. God uses the religions to teach the church deeper insight into the meaning of Christ and the biblical deposit of truth. We have mentioned how the early church used Greek philosophical religion to better understand and articulate the Trinity. This pattern continued through church history. Augustine, for example, was aided by Plotinus and his Neoplatonic ontology (his understanding of being, influenced by Plato) to understand evil as lacking in substance, to break from Manichaeanism (a Gnostic sect based on a supposed primeval conflict between light and darkness) by seeing the biblical emphasis on God's sovereignty and holiness, and to battle Donatism (schismatic part of the fourth-century African church that refused to accept sacraments from priests who had surrendered during the persecutions but later repented) by seeing that the church on earth will never be a company of the perfected.

It wasn't only Augustine. Thanks to (the pagan) Aristotle's embrace of nature, Thomas Aquinas gained confidence to articulate a biblical doctrine of the resurrection of the body in an age that demeaned corporality. Aristotle also helped Aquinas develop his concept of analogy, which ever since has helped Christians understand how they can talk about an infinite God using broken, finite language. Even John Calvin was helped to better understand biblical revelation by pagan thinking. Renaissance humanism's celebration of rhetoric helped Calvin see the importance of preaching. Its confidence in self-reformation through human effort may have stimulated Calvin's notable formulation of what we call sanctification, and its conception of oratory as deliberately attuned to the ears of an audience helped shape Calvin's classic portrayal of how God accommodates his message to "mean" human capacities."[1]

What Are the Religions?

The answers we have just looked at lead to another question: What *are* the religions? Or, to put it another way, if God permitted them because of his respect for our freedom, even when we choose distortions of his revelation, doesn't that suggest that all non-Christian religion is distor-

---

[1]For a fuller argument on how Augustine, Aquinas and Calvin learned from other religious sources, see Gerald R. McDermott, *Can Evangelicals Learn from World Religions? Jesus, Revelation & Religious Traditions* (Downers Grove, Ill.: InterVarsity Press, 2000), chap. 5.

tion? If so, where did the distortions and therefore the religions come from? And if not, how can there be truth in what is a distortion of the truth?[2]

Again, the preceding chapters had a lot to say to answer these questions—often directly, sometimes indirectly. Here I will sum up what we have seen. There is a line of teaching in both biblical Testaments that non-Jewish and non-Christian religions were inspired by divine powers that were created good but then went bad. As Paul suggested, angelic powers rebelled in pride against their Maker and enticed whole populations to worship them instead of the Father of Jesus Christ. They distorted what they knew of God's truth and held their devotees in a kind of bondage to a version of divine law. Hence the religions were born in deception and malice.

But at the same time the religions are tutors of a sort. God uses their very distortions to teach truth by the very mixture they produce. Their truth, mixed with error, was sown by seeds from the Logos. That truth keeps people from ruining their lives by wholesale avoidance of God's law, and it leads some to a reverent fear of God.

As Clement put it most clearly, the religions demonstrate various adaptations of a mixture of truth and error to an infinite variety of historical conditions. The Fall demonstrated that every human being and culture turns away from God's truth, and that ever new mixtures of truth and error result from a variety of human dispositions. Human cultures have created alternative religions in response both to divine revelation in nature and conscience and to the mixed teachings of fallen angelic powers. God did not abandon human beings, however, to error and rebellion. Instead, out of love for every culture and person, by means of the Logos he sprinkled seeds of truth and even prophets (though quite different from the biblical prophets) among the new religions—lest too many would be utterly lost.

This is why the religions are a mixed bag and cannot save. They contain broken and refracted traces of revelation, not the fullness of revela-

---

[2]The same of course can be asked about Christianity. If there has been false teaching and misunderstanding, how can we know there is truth? The answer to this question is similar to the answer to that about the religions—Jesus and the apostolic tradition give us a rule by which to measure all claims to truth.

tion that is in the gospel. They have only reflections of light, not the light itself. They are like the moon rather than the sun. In sum, they contain hints and shadows that participate in the Logos. But in the Christian revelation one can see and be joined to the Logos himself.

Before we close this section, let me answer a question you may have: Are we required by the biblical revelation to believe that the religions were literally started by fallen angels? I don't think so. This notion of angels and powers at the root of the religions is most certainly in the Bible, but its delineation is never crystal clear. As we have seen, the Bible's construal of religious origins varies from Old to New Testament, and even within each testament. The early Fathers sound more sure of the precise shape of these origins than the biblical authors seem to have been. So while we are free to be agnostic about the specific contours of religious beginnings—angelic or demonic or something else—we cannot deny the biblical insistence that the religions are as much supernatural as natural. That is, not only are human beings at work in other faiths but also real spiritual powers. Moreover, God as well as the devil is present in the religions. Of course, when we look at the history of Christianity, we must say the same for *it*. If God inspired the Reformation and St. Francis of Assisi, the devil was close at hand during the Inquisition and "Christian" slavery. As Christians we must acknowledge that the fullness of truth is in Jesus Christ, but also that we never come close to possessing that fullness. Other religions lack access to that fullness not only because they reject Christ's most central claims but also because they teach things in conflict with Christ's claims. But while we have access to the fullness of Christ, our own openness to the devil prevents us from seeing that fullness. So does the church's limited understanding of that fullness.

Implications: Where Do We Go from Here?

If all of the above is so, or even just close to being so, what are we to make of it? What difference will it make to what we think about God and the world?

Let me suggest a number of ways in which this new understanding should change the way we think. First and most obviously, it should change the way we think about the religions. They aren't just human creations, but they may also involve real cosmic powers. This should change the way we think about our friends and neighbors who practice other religions. They are involved not simply with human constructions but real spiritual entities. These entities may have been originally created by God to praise him and further his kingdom. Even if they later rebelled, they still retain and teach truth in the midst of distortions. And they are used by God, in God's own sovereign plan, to serve the ends of redemption, even though at one level, and for all that we can see, the religions seem to resist God's purposes.[3]

This also means that other religionists are not our enemies. And we should not fight them. Our real battle, as Paul advises us, is not against human beings—flesh and blood—but against "the cosmic powers of this present darkness" (Eph 6:12). If we have any enemies besides sin, flesh and the devil, it is the cosmic powers that war against God's kingdom and that sometimes use other religions to mask their designs. (They also wage war within the church, often pitting Christian believer against Christian believer!) Even if we do war against cosmic powers that sometimes use other religions, our weapons should be spiritual, not worldly. "For the weapons of our warfare are not fleshly" (2 Cor 10:4, my trans.).

That believers of other religions are not our enemy means patient persuasion, not hostile argument. It means loving witness to others who sincerely believe they have the truth. We may believe they have been deceived by spiritual forces, but we must first acknowledge that we don't have complete possession of the full truth either. No doubt we are also deceived to some extent—even though we know that Christian faith is the final reality to which all other faiths should eventually lead. Having access to the true God through Christ does not mean complete possession of the truth since we are finite and sinners, belonging to a church

---

[3]Some Christians think that if there are any supernatural elements in non-Christian religions, the only proper response is exorcism. But this is faulty for two reasons. First, Paul's admonition to "take up the whole armor of God" against the "cosmic powers" means employing "truth," "righteousness," "faith" and "prayer"—in other words, ordinary tools for daily encounters with people of other faiths (Eph 6:10-20). One can and should pray against the "cosmic powers" that distort truth, but Paul suggests that the principal work will look like any other kind of work with people, yet animated by "peace" and loving "righteousness" (Eph 6:14-15). The second problem with the exorcism-first-and-primarily position is that it typically assumes that the "cosmic powers" are more common in the "religious" than other (say, political, social and economic) domains.

that is still growing in its understanding of Christ.

This likewise means that we need to share the gospel with more respect and sensitivity. If our non-Christian friends and neighbors sense that we believe their religious traditions contain religious truth, they may be more open to what we have to say. They won't feel they have to deny everything they have ever believed and practiced in order to become a disciple of Jesus, or that their culture has had no value in their religious pilgrimage. They will have a better chance of feeling love and respect from the Christian sharing her story.

It also means that we have a lot in common with believers of other religions. We agree with them that final reality is spiritual, not material.[4] We agree with many of them—Muslims, for example—that God is moral and that he has given us divine law. In fact, this understanding of the powers, as we have seen above, reinforces the idea that we must submit to moral law. It is for this reason that Catholics could work side-by-side with Muslims at the 1995 United Nations Conference on Population and Development in Cairo to prevent abortion-on-demand from being enshrined as a universal human right. It is why Christians and Muslims can work together today to defend marriage. They, along with believers from other religious traditions, agree with Christians that this world is the creation of God and that one day all of us will be judged. They agree that God is just and good. And this commonality in knowledge about God and his ways helps restrain sin and evil in us all, so that the world is a happier place than it would be without these religions.

If this new understanding will change the ways we think about other believers, it may also change the way we think about Christ. As we saw toward the beginning of this chapter (recall Augustine, Thomas Aquinas and Calvin), God has often used other religions to help his people better understand Christ and his gospel. We saw this even in the Bible (chapter two). It may be that some of today's religions portray aspects of the divine mystery that the Bible does not equally emphasize: for example, the Qur'an's sense of the divine majesty and transcendence, as well as the human being's submission to the holiness of God's eternal decrees.

---

[4]But final reality involves heavenly matter, as it were, for we look forward not to a purely spiritual heaven in the clouds but to "the new heavens and the new earth" (Rev 21—22).

Hindu traditions can help remind Christians of God's immanence when deistic tendencies have obscured it. Theravadin Buddhists may be able to show us dimensions of the fallen ego that will shed greater light on what Paul meant by "the old man." Philosophical Daoists may have insights into nonaction that can help Christians better understand "waiting on God." Confucius's portrayal of virtue may open new understandings of radical discipleship, and the Qur'an's attention to the physical world's "signs" of God's reality can enrich our belief that the cosmos is the theater of God's glory.[5]

I am not saying that these are new insights not presently taught by the biblical revelation. They are in the Bible, either explicitly or implicitly. But many of us in the church have not seen them, or we see them less clearly than we could. God can use other religions to help us see what he put there long ago—just as he used Greek philosophy to help Christians in the first three centuries see with some clarity the biblical data about God being both one and three. Or think of the way God used Neoplatonism to show Augustine things about Christ that he and the church had not previously seen. And the way God used Aristotle to shed light for Thomas Aquinas on certain aspects of Christ and life with him. As George Lindbeck has argued, other religions can teach Christians just as geocentrists taught heliocentrists certain things, even though the latter knew the former were wrong in their overall interpretation of the data.[6]

The Spirit can also use other religions to judge and purify the church. God can use devotees of other faiths to show us Christians—if we are open to it—the poverty of our own commitment. We may also see or hear God in the encounter. Some missionaries report there is frequently a moment in missions when the missionary realizes that those being evangelized may already implicitly or explicitly know God (as the early Fathers would put it, they have already heard the voice of the Logos, even if they do not possess the fullness of the Logos), and that from such persons the Christian may hear God's word—even as Peter learned from Cornelius's religious experience and heard God's word through him.

---

[5]For further explication of these points, see McDermott, *Can Evangelicals Learn from World Religions?* chaps. 6-9.

[6]George A. Lindbeck, *The Nature of Doctrine: Religion and Theology in a Postliberal Age* (Philadelphia: Westminster Press, 1984), p. 67.

At the same time, a yellow caution flag should be raised. Mature believers (who are not necessarily older in years) can discern truth from error in the religions. But younger believers are often confused. When we realize that a real spiritual power may be animating a particular religion or certain dimensions of it and there is therefore the danger of a spiritual "pull" that transcends intellectual and other kinds of attractions, we should warn less discerning believers to exercise caution. Those young in faith should spend more energy learning from Scripture, theology and fellowship than investigating the intricacies of other traditions. Serious study of other religions is better after deep spiritual and theological roots have had time to thicken.

We are also reminded by these reflections from the Bible and the early Fathers that other religions do not provide a road of salvation to the triune God. If believers in other religions are saved, it is only by the work of Christ in his perfect life and death. And it is also through their acceptance of the gospel. We don't know how God does that in many cases. Perhaps, as some of the Fathers suggested, the creed's assertion that Christ went to Hades to preach the gospel is the symbol that in some mysterious way Christ presents the gospel at or after death to those who have not yet heard. In any event, no one will be judged unjustly, for we know that God is just and good.

If this study sheds light on Christian salvation, it should also enlarge our view of God. As the Fathers argued, God has always been at work in every human culture, but always by the Word, the Logos. This makes sense to the Christian believer who reads in the sacred text that God "desires everyone to be saved and to come to the knowledge of the truth" (1 Tim 2:4). Other religions may be inspired in part by other powers, but God has not abandoned whole cultures to perdition and untruth. God is still at work, using even distorted truth to teach truth. And his Spirit is still actively leading individuals within the religions to draw closer to himself.

Appendix

God and the Masculine Pronoun

I MUST EXPLAIN WHY I USE THE MASCULINE PRONOUN for God when some Christians argue that such use renders God sexual and diminishes the worth of females.[1] These are important concerns and need to be taken seriously. Feminists make an important point when they argue that masculine language for God should not be used to the exclusion of all feminine imagery. The Bible itself uses feminine imagery (Num 11:12; Ps 22:9-10; 71:6; 139:13; Is 49:15; 66:9,13; Mt 23:37); use of feminine imagery and language in prayer will surely enrich our apprehension of God's self-giving love.

But when it is suggested that the masculine pronoun for God be excised because of women's oppression by men, the cure proves worse than the disease. Avoidance of the masculine pronoun for God often forces us to use ungainly expressions like "Godself," which is not only awkward but also theologically problematic because it undermines the notion that God is a person. It is particularly important to highlight God's personhood when discussing religions that deny it. Philosophical Hindus and Buddhists, for example, insist there is no personal God because there is no final distinction between God and the cosmos.

Second, avoidance of the masculine pronoun reminds me of Stanley Hauerwas's response to John Cobb's portrayal of what Cobb calls Christian progressivism: "One of the things that bothers me about John Cobb's

---

[1]This essay is adapted from a similar one in Gerald R. McDermott, *Can Evangelicals Learn from World Religions? Jesus, Revelation and Religious Traditions* (Downers Grove, Ill.: InterVarsity Press, 2000).

God is that she is just too damn nice."[2] The problem with "Godself" is that "it" is too inoffensive, and as a result assumes too much. It runs the risk of avoiding the scandal of particularity (the Christian God is the Father who sent his Son to die on Pilate's cross), and it suggests that we can know the divine essence behind the biblical Father, Son and Holy Spirit. But Scripture tells us that we know the Father truly only through the Son (Mt 11:27; 1 Jn 2:23), and the creeds inform us that God is known first not as some amorphous essence but as Father.[3] In other words, we don't know anything about any god but the God who has revealed himself as Father, Son and Holy Spirit. We don't know a supposed divine essence behind the Father and Son that can be named without the name Father and Son. All we know is that God has given us his name as Father, Son and Holy Spirit. And when God alone is invoked by Scripture, that God is the "Father." Hence "Father" and "Son" are not simply metaphorical but literal names—indeed proper names—of the deity.[4]

If God is Trinity—a Trinity of Father, Son and Holy Spirit—there is no way to avoid the *suggestion* of gender. For the words "Father" and "Son" both connote maleness. Those who keep the language of the Trinity but refuse to use the masculine pronoun cannot have it both ways. They think that in order to protect their insistence that God has no gender they must avoid the masculine pronoun. But when they use "Father" and "Son" language, they still suggest gender, and they must explain that this suggestion of gender is relativized by God's transcendence. Yet this argument is no different from mine: While I use language *suggesting* maleness—as we humans understand it—the revelation of the Trinity shows that its maleness is radically different (as Garrett Green argues below). Hence those who retain Trinitarian language but avoid the masculine pronoun have the same theological problem as those who use the masculine pronoun. The problem of gender cannot be resolved linguistically

---

[2]Stanley Hauerwas, "Knowing How to Go On When You Do Not Know Where You Are," *Theology Today* 51, no. 4 (January 1995): 567.

[3]"The Apostles' Creed does not begin with the divine essence but with the Person of the Father: 'I believe in God, the Father almighty.' The Nicene Creed does not make God first *ousia* but *hypostasis*, not essence first but person: 'I believe in one God, the Father almighty.'" Patrick Henry Reardon, "Father, Glorify Thy Name," *Pro Ecclesia* 7, no. 2 (Spring 1998): 143.

[4]Robert W. Jenson, "The Father, He . . . ," in *Speaking the Christian God: The Holy Trinity and the Challenge of Feminism,* ed. Alvin E. Kimel Jr. (Grand Rapids: Eerdmans, 1992), pp. 95-109.

without sacrificing the heart of the Christian faith. That is, only by removing all Trinitarian language can all suggestion of gender be eliminated. But then one is left with a god quite different from the divine reality of Jesus Christ.

Therefore use of the masculine pronoun for the Christian God is necessary because God cannot be truly known apart from his revelation in Christ. As Luther put it, to try to know God apart from the historical particularity of the Son and his cross is to construct a theology of glory. Similarly, avoiding the masculine pronoun suggests that we can know God apart from the revelation that God is the Father of the Son. Hence they cannot be replaced. They are not human constructions in response to ineffable religious experiences, but names for God given to humans by God himself. The very names encapsulate the entire story of the triune God. To avoid them is to suggest indirectly that God did not reveal himself as a Father to a Son, or at least that these are not divinely given names.

Does this mean that God is male? Of course not. And the best representatives of the grand tradition have always agreed. "No one in the whole conciliar and creedal tradition regarded the word 'father,' when used in reference to God, as having any sexual connotation whatsoever. The Cappadocians in particular had already gone to some length to say that paternity and sonship in God possessed no sexual reference."[5]

Must we do something about the misperceptions of God and the oppression of women to which these misperceptions have contributed? Yes, but the way to go is not to reject the name and thus the masculine pronoun that follows, but rather to correct the distortions of readings that assume a male gender. This involves correcting the assumption of "metaphorical theology" (that assumes that all language for God is simply metaphorical and thus can be changed without doing untoward damage to meaning) that Trinitarian "Father" and "Son" language simply extends ordinary understanding of "father" and "son" to God. But the biblical authors assumed meaning flows not from the bottom up but from the top down. Paul wrote in Ephesians that all fatherhood on earth derives its name and meaning from God's fatherhood (Eph 3:15). The

---

[5]Reardon, "Father, Glorify Thy Name," p. 148.

same dynamic is found in divine Sonship, according to C. S. Lewis: "Divine Sonship is, so to speak, the solid of which biological sonship is merely a diagrammatic representation on the flat."[6] In other words, we are to draw a proper conception of "father" and "son" from the Trinity, as revealed to us, rather than understanding the Trinity from our experience of human families.[7]

Garrett Green argues that another failing of metaphorical theology is its tendency to treat metaphors atomistically—out of context. If we attend to the story from which Father and Son come, we find a God very different from the one vilified by some of those who oppose the masculine pronoun for God.

> *This* God does not jealously hoard his power. As husband he does not beat his unfaithful wife but cries out with the pain of a jilted lover and redoubles his efforts to win her back. As Father he does not spare his own son but gave him up for us all. As Son he did not claim the prerogatives of power and lord it over his subjects but emptied himself, taking the form of a servant—and humbled himself on a shameful cross. As Spirit he incorporates us into the mystical body of Christ, in whom there is neither slave nor free, male nor female. As king he does not isolate himself in heavenly splendor but wills to dwell with his people, to wipe away every tear from their eyes and to deliver them from all that oppresses them, even death itself.[8]

Green concludes, "Anyone who claims that masculine metaphors . . . are 'oppressive to women' is interpreting them out of context, treating them as isolated units of meaning rather than integral elements of a living narrative."[9]

According to Ellen Charry, men who abuse women have perverted

---

[6]C. S. Lewis, *Miracles* (New York: Macmillan, 1947), from chap. 11, "Christianity and 'Religion.'"

[7]In a superb essay on God-language, Gary Deddo argues that if indeed we are dependent on our own experience for our understanding of God, then we can never have any assurance of knowledge of God because all of our experience is broken to some degree. See Deddo, "Jesus' Paradigm for Relating Human Experience and Language About God," in *Unapologetic Apologetics: Meeting the Challenges of Theological Studies,* ed. William A. Dembski and Jay Wesley Richards (Downers Grove, Ill.: InterVarsity Press, 2001), pp. 187-206.

[8]Garrett Green, "The Gender of God and the Theology of Metaphor," in *Speaking the Christian God: The Holy Trinity and the Challenge of Feminism,* ed. Alvin E. Kimel Jr. (Grand Rapids: Eerdmans, 1992), p. 60.

[9]Ibid.

notions of fatherhood and sonship, which a proper understanding of the Trinity can help correct: "If men have identified manliness with an understanding of divine fatherhood and sonship that reinforces their own proclivities to control, subjugate, or wreak violence upon others to bolster their own feelings of power, they have gerrymandered the Christian doctrine of the Trinity, the reason for the incarnation, the power of the cross, and the hope of resurrection." Hence to eliminate Trinitarian language is to deprive the church of its "primary models" for correcting these distortions.[10]

Therefore I use the masculine pronoun for God so as not to distract readers from the biblical narrative that alone reveals the true God who is neither patriarchalist nor culturally fashionable. He is the terrifying Other who explodes our ideas about him—whether they be that he is male or that he is culturally inoffensive.

---

[10]Ellen Charry, "Is Christianity Good for Us?" in *Reclaiming Faith: Essays on Orthodoxy in the Episcopal Church and the Baltimore Declaration,* ed. Ephraim Radner and George R. Sumner (Grand Rapids: Eerdmans, 1993), p. 234. For another excellent essay on God-language, see Katherine Greene-McCreight, "What's in a Name? On the Ecumenical Baptismal Formula," *Pro Ecclesia* 6, no. 3 (summer 1997): 289-308.

Author and Subject Index

Scripture Index

3m